Objective-C

P H R A S E B O O K

SECOND EDITION

David Chisnall

✦Addison-Wesley   **DEVELOPER'S LIBRARY**

Upper Saddle River, NJ · Boston · Indianapolis · San Francisco
New York · Toronto · Montreal · London · Munich · Paris · Madrid
Cape Town · Sydney · Tokyo · Singapore · Mexico City

Library of Congress Cataloging-in-Publication Data is on file.

Copyright © 2012 Pearson Education, Inc.

ISBN-13: 978-0-321-81375-6
ISBN-10: 0-321-81375-8

Text printed in the United States on recycled paper at RR Donnelly in Crawfordsville, Indiana.

First printing October 2011

Editor-in-Chief Mark Taub	**Managing Editor** Kristy Hart	**Proofreader** Charlotte Kughen	**Cover Designer** Gary Adair
Acquisitions Editor Mark Taber	**Project Editor** Anne Goebel	**Publishing Coordinator** Vanessa Evans	**Senior Compositor** Gloria Schurick
Development Editor Michael Thurston	**Copy Editor** Bart Reed		

Table of Contents

About the Author

David Chisnall is a freelance writer and consultant. While studying for his PhD, he co-founded the Étoilé project, which aims to produce an open-source desktop environment on top of GNUstep, an open-source implementation of the OpenStep and Cocoa APIs. He is an active contributor to GNUstep and is the original author and maintainer of the GNUstep Objective-C 2 runtime library and the associated compiler support in the Clang compiler.

After completing his PhD, David hid in academia for a while, studying the history of programming languages. He finally escaped when he realized that there were places off campus with an equally good view of the sea and without the requirement to complete quite so much paperwork. He occasionally returns to collaborate on projects involving modeling the semantics of dynamic languages.

David has a great deal of familiarity with Objective-C, having worked both on projects using the language and on implementing the language itself. He has also worked on implementing other languages, including dialects of Smalltalk and JavaScript, on top of an Objective-C runtime, allowing mixing code between all of these languages without bridging.

When not writing or programming, David enjoys dancing Argentine Tango and Cuban Salsa, playing badminton and ultimate frisbee, and cooking.

Acknowledgments

When writing a book about Objective-C, the first person I should thank is Nicolas Roard. I got my first Mac at around the same time I started my PhD and planned to use it to write Java code, not wanting to learn a proprietary language. When I started my PhD, I found myself working with Nicolas, who was an active GNUstep contributor. He convinced me that Objective-C and Cocoa were not just for Macs and that they were both worth learning. He was completely right: Objective-C is a wonderfully elegant language, and the accompanying frameworks make development incredibly easy.

The next person to thank is Fred Kiefer. Fred is the maintainer of the GNUstep implementation of the AppKit framework. He did an incredibly thorough (read: pedantic) technical review of this book, finding several places where things were not explained as well as they could have been. If you enjoy reading this book, then Fred deserves a lot of the credit.

Finally, I need to thank everyone else who was involved in bringing this book from my text editor to your hands, especially Mark Taber who originally proposed the idea to me.

We Want to Hear from You

As the reader of this book, *you* are our most important critic and commentator. We value your opinion and want to know what we're doing right, what we could do better, what areas you'd like to see us publish in, and any other words of wisdom you're willing to pass our way.

You can email or write me directly to let me know what you did or didn't like about this book—as well as what we can do to make our books stronger.

Please note that I cannot help you with technical problems related to the topic of this book, and that due to the high volume of mail I receive, I might not be able to reply to every message.

When you write, please be sure to include this book's title and author as well as your name and phone or email address. I will carefully review your comments and share them with the author and editors who worked on the book.

E-mail:	mark.taber@pearson.com
Mail:	Mark Taber
	Associate Publisher
	Addison Wesley Publishing
	800 East 96th Street
	Indianapolis, IN 46240 USA

Reader Services

Visit our website and register this book at informit.com/aw for convenient access to any updates, downloads, or errata that might be available for this book.

Introduction

Blaise Pascal once wrote, "I didn't have time to write a short letter, so I wrote a long one instead." This phrasebook is the shortest book I've written, and trying to fit everything that I wanted to say into a volume this short was a challenge.

When Mark Taber originally suggested that I write an Objective-C Phrasebook, I was not sure what it would look like. A phrasebook for a natural language is a list of short idioms that can be used by people who find themselves in need of a quick sentence or two. A phrasebook for a programming language should fulfil a similar rôle.

This book is not a language reference. Apple provides a competent reference for the Objective-C language on the `http://developer.apple.com` site. This is not a detailed tutorial; unlike my other Objective-C book, *Cocoa Programming Developer's Handbook*, you won't find complete programs as code examples. Instead, you'll find very short examples of Objective-C idioms, which hopefully you can employ in a wide range of places.

One of the most frustrating things in life is finding that code examples in a book don't actually work. There are two sorts of code listings in this book. Code on a white background is intended to illustrate a simple point. This code may depend on some implied context and should not be taken as working, usable examples.

The majority of the code you will find in this book is on a gray background. At the bottom of each of these examples, you will find the name of the file that the listing was taken from. You can download these from the book's page on InformIT's website: `http://www.informit.com/title/0321743628`

When I wrote the first edition of this book, I wrote and tested all of the examples on OS X. After sending the draft manuscript off for editing, I tested them on GNUstep and was pleasantly surprised that almost all of them worked. By the time the book was published, they all worked. The second edition covers a number of features that are only supported by Apple on Mac OS X 10.7 or iOS 5. All of these examples also work with GNUstep. As before, I have written all of the examples on OS X, without making any concessions for GNUstep other than testing the examples there.

A Note About Typesetting

This book was written in Vim, using semantic markup. From here, three different versions are generated. Two are created using pdflatex. If you are reading either the printed or PDF version, then you can see one of these. The only difference between the two is that the print version contains crop marks to allow the printer to trim the pages.

The third version is XHTML, intended for the ePub edition. This is created using the EtoileText framework, which first parses the LaTeX-style markup to a tree structure, then performs some transformations for handling cross-references and indexing, and finally generates XHTML. The code for doing this is all written in Objective-C.

If you have access to both, you may notice that the code listings look slightly nicer in the ePub edition. This is because EtoileText uses SourceCodeKit, another Étoilé framework, for syntax highlighting. This uses part of Clang, a modern Objective-C compiler, to mark up the code listings. This means that ranges of the code are annotated with exactly the same semantic types that the compiler sees. For example, it can distinguish between a function call and a macro instantiation.

You can find all of the code for doing this in the Étoilé subversion repository: `http://svn.gna.org/viewcvs/etoile/trunk/Etoile/`

The Objective-C Philosophy

To understand Objective-C, you need to understand the philosophy behind its creation. Unlike C++, D, or Java, which were designed to be new, C-like languages, Objective-C is a hybrid language. It is a pure superset of C, meaning that every valid C program is also a valid Objective-C program, but it also allows some Smalltalk-like syntax and semantics.

One of the designers of Objective-C, Tom Love, described the square bracket syntax as a signpost reminding you that you were leaving C and entering "object land." The original idea behind Objective-C was a way of packaging C libraries that encouraged loose coupling between components.

One of the fundamental design decisions in Objective-C was that there should be no magic. All of the details of the implementation are exposed to the programmer. Unlike C++, where the details of the vtable are private, Objective-C lets you inspect and modify everything about objects and classes.

With older runtime libraries, Objective-C classes were represented by C structures with a public definition. You could modify them directly, or even create new ones and register them with the runtime system. With newer ones, these structures are private and there is a set of public functions for manipulating them as opaque types.

Understanding the Object Model

Objective-C has a Smalltalk-like object model. If you come from Java, you will find this very easy to understand. If you come from a Simula-family language, such as C++, you may find it a bit more difficult.

Alan Kay described the idea of objects as a simple exercise in reduction. When solving a problem, you want to decompose it into simple parts. The simplest thing that can run a part of a program is the same thing that can run the whole of a program: a computer. Objects, in Alan Kay's vision, are simple models of computers that communicate by exchanging messages.

This is exactly how objects in Objective-C, and its parent Smalltalk, behave. They are isolated parts of a program that pass messages between each other. Typically, these messages are delivered synchronously, so they behave a bit like a function call, but it's important to realize that they are different.

Messages are a higher level of abstraction than function calls. A function call is very simple. On many architectures it is a single instruction. On more RISC-like architectures, you push the return address onto the stack and then jump. In all cases, the destination address is fixed.

When you send a message, it is entirely up to the receiver how to handle it. The most typical way is to invoke the method with the same name as the message, but there are other alternatives. Proxy objects may forward the message to another object, and they may perform some substitution on the message arguments before they do.

Simula did not use the term "object orientation," but a lot of Simula-like languages that postdate Smalltalk have adopted the term, leading to some confusion. Languages in this family, such as C++, use *virtual function tables (vtables)* to implement something that is superficially similar.

A Simula-style object contains a pointer to its vtable, or vtables if it has superclasses. When you call a virtual function, the compiler creates an offset into the vtable and then a call to the function at this offset.

One of the side effects of this difference is

that pointer casting in Objective-C and C++ have very different semantics. When you cast a pointer to one object type to another in Objective-C, no code is generated. The cast is just a hint to the compiler's type checker. In C++, however, a pointer cast performs some pointer arithmetic so that code that is passed the cast pointer can find the vtable at the correct location. This means that you can cast any object type to any other object type in Objective-C, whereas in C++ you need to use a special kind of cast.

This distinction is very important. In Objective-C, the only thing that affects the method lookup is the type of the object. In C++ and other Simula-family languages, the lookup is also affected by what the compiler thinks the type of the object is.

A Tale of Two Type Systems

One of the things that can confuse people coming to Objective-C is that it has two type systems. This makes sense if you consider the original implementation as a preprocessor. The Objective-C preprocessor would perform Strongtalk-like[1] type checking and then the C

---

[1]StrongTalk is a dialect of Smalltalk that adds optional static type checking. The team that created the language later went to work on Java. StrongTalk was the fastest Smalltalk implementations, but the compiler did not use static type information for optimization.

compiler would perform C type checking.

C has a structural type system. Type equivalence for primitive types is based on whether two types have the same representation. Complex types are never regarded as equivalent.

Objective-C adds an algebraic type system. The type of an object is defined by its signature: the messages that it claims it will respond to. You can implicitly cast an Objective-C object to its superclass, because it is guaranteed to respond to all of the messages that the superclass understands.

You can explicitly cast objects to other types. You could, for example, cast a dictionary object to an array object. As long as you then only send it messages that are understood by both dictionaries and arrays, this will work.

C Is Objective-C

One of the most important features of Objective-C is that it is a pure superset of C. You can think of C as a domain-specific language embedded in Objective-C for low-level tasks and a subset of Smalltalk as a domain-specific language embedded in Objective-C for high-level tasks.

There is nothing wrong with solving a problem using pure C. One of the mistakes that a lot of people make when learning Objective-C is to assume that they must stop using C. For a lot of things, the C solution is the correct one.

Note: Objective-C also has a sister language, Objective-C++, which has the same relationship to C++ that Objective-C has to C. Objective-C++ is a pure superset of C++ and allows you to call C++ code from Objective-C objects, and vice versa. Because they have very different object models, you cannot subclass an Objective-C class with C++, or the converse; however, you can use pointers to Objective-C objects as fields in C++ objects and pointers to C++ objects as instance variables in Objective-C objects.

You can see this in the Cocoa frameworks. Not everything is an object. If you ask for a range of characters in a string, you will use an **NSRange** structure. This is a C structure—not an Objective-C object—containing a location and a length. Points, rectangles, and several other things are represented in a similar way. If these were objects, then you would use more memory, make manipulating them slower, and not really gain any flexibility.

The Ingalls test[2] for object orientation says that you should be able to create a new kind of integer and use this in positioning a window on the screen. Objective-C fails this test, but it's not a very useful example in the real world, because most of the time designing new kinds of

---

[2]Named after Dan Ingalls, one of the designers of Smalltalk, who proposed it.

integers would break a lot of things that expect integers to have the standard behavior.

In Objective-C, you don't have to use the dynamic behavior, such as late binding and polymorphism, in cases where it isn't useful.

The Language and the Library

It's difficult with very dynamic languages to draw the line between the language and the library. In Smalltalk, there is no equivalent of an **if** statement in the language. The standard library defines **True** and **False** singleton classes, which respond to **-ifTrue:** messages taking a closure as an argument. All complex flow control structures, such as loops or enumeration, are implemented in terms of this.

Objective-C inherits flow control from C, but all of the dynamic behavior is supplied by the runtime library. This is different from C or C++. You can compile a freestanding C or C++ binary that doesn't call any functions in libc or libstdc++. Every Objective-C program that isn't a pure C program, however, must link against libobjc to work.

This library traditionally provides three classes: a simple root class, a class for constant strings, and a class for protocols. The first of these provides functionality including object allocation that is part of the language in C++, Java, and similar environments. The other two are classes that may be generated by the compiler.

Most of the time, you will not use any of these classes. Almost all Objective-C code written in the last decade or two uses an implementation of the OpenStep Foundation framework. OpenStep was a specification jointly worked out by NeXT and Sun to provide a modern object-oriented framework for cross-platform application development. NeXT implemented it on their OPENSTEP operating system and on Windows NT, whereas Sun shipped an implementation for Solaris. A little bit later, the GNU project shipped a third implementation: GNUstep.

OpenStep defined two frameworks: the Foundation Kit and Application Kit, typically shortened to Foundation and AppKit. The Foundation Kit provides the core functionality that developers need for all applications, such as collection classes, run loops, notification delivery, OS abstraction, and so on. The Application Kit is built on top of this and provides extra support for building graphical applications.

Sun's implementation didn't see much development after the initial release. Apple bought NeXT a few years later and renamed the OpenStep environment Yellow Box, shipping it as a developer environment both in Rhapsody and on Windows. With the release of OS X, it was renamed yet again, this time to Cocoa.

The GNUstep project is still actively developed, but now tracks Apple's enhancements to the

OpenStep specification, as well as the core specification. This means that the Foundation framework is usable pretty much anywhere, although some of the newest classes and methods are missing with the GNUstep implementation.

You can think of the Foundation framework as the Objective-C standard library. It provides a lot of features that are required for nontrivial programs. Several of the Objective-C 2 features are designed specifically to work with Foundation. You can use them without Foundation, but only if you implement something equivalent.

The History of Objective-C

The term "object oriented" was coined by Alan Kay in the 1960s, and Smalltalk was the language that he and others created to demonstrate this style of programming. Smalltalk was developed during the 1970s, with the most widespread version being released in 1980.

Smalltalk, however, was very slow. To run it properly, you needed a powerful computer such as the Xerox Alto, with 512KB of RAM and ideally at least a 2MHz processor.

Brad Cox liked the idea of Smalltalk, but wanted a language that he could use on computers that people could afford. His idea was to marry Smalltalk, a high-level language encouraging encapsulation, loose coupling, and code reuse, with C. C was right at the other end of the

spectrum, with little by way of encapsulation, no
dynamic dispatch, but with one big advantage:
It was fast.

C was based heavily on the PDP-11 instruction
set. A very naive C compiler could produce quite
fast code. This is true even today. Compilers
such as LLVM, XLC, and ICC put a lot of effort
into optimization, but PCC, which does almost
none, still produces reasonably fast code.

Brad Cox and Tom Love set up StepStone in
1986, selling a product based on Brad's earlier
Object Oriented Precompiler. This product,
Objective-C, was a preprocessor and a small
Objective-C runtime library. The preprocessor
generated C code that you could compile with
your platform's C compiler. As recently as
2010, I came across a company still using the
StepStone compiler in a commercial product.

In 1988, NeXT bought a license to StepStone's
code and bought the Objective-C trademark
outright. NeXT then rewrote the preprocessor
as a front end to the *GNU Compiler Collection
(GCC).* After some legal wrangling, the Free
Software Foundation forced them to release this
code, but they kept the runtime library private.

The GNU project then wrote a replacement for
the runtime library, but made some changes.
One was that selectors in the GNU runtime
had a type associated with them. On NeXT
(and Apple) platforms, selectors are just strings.
This means that the GNU runtime can catch,

at run time, some stack corruption caused by programmer errors that are invisible to the NeXT runtime.

The other change was in how message sending works. When you send a message with the NeXT runtime, the compiler turns the message send into a call to the `objc_msgSend()` function. This looks up the method and then calls it. Unfortunately, it is not possible to implement this function in C. It has to be written in assembly for every platform and for every calling convention on that platform. The GNU solution was to replace this with a `objc_msg_lookup()` function, which returns a pointer to the function. This is slightly slower, but means that the same code can work on all platforms.

Objective-C didn't change much from this point. NeXT was purchased by Apple in 1997 and Objective-C adopted as the primary development language for the Yellow Box on their new Rhapsody operating system. These were later renamed Cocoa and OS X, respectively. In 2003, Apple added some Java-like exception handling primitives to the language.

The next set of upgrades came in 2007, when Apple introduced Objective-C 2. This was slightly confusing to older Objective-C programmers, because the previous version—the one that NeXT had shipped—had been Objective-C 4. Fortunately, the belief that 2 is the number immediately following 4 does not seem to have made its way into any of the sorting code in Cocoa.

Objective-C 2 added a few bits of syntactic sugar. It provided a new way of doing enumeration, a way of synthesizing accessor methods, and introduced *garbage collection*. Objective-C 2 is more of a marketing buzzword than a real language. You won't find a compiler switch for selecting it. Some of the features, such as non-fragile instance variables, are only available on some runtimes. Others, such as garbage collection, are not available on the iPhone. Declared properties and fast enumeration are the only Objective-C 2 features that work everywhere, including non-Apple platforms.

With iOS 5 and Mac OS X 10.7, Apple moved away from version numbers and started using compiler versions to describe features. Prior to release, the set of new features were known as Objective-C 2.1, but Apple's marketing division decided not to use this name publicly. These new features included some better support for data hiding, making it easier to move implementation details out of public headers, and automatic reference counting, which combines most— but not quite all—of the benefits of garbage collection and manual reference counting, without most of the disadvantages of either.

Cross-Platform Support

Forcing NeXT to release the Objective-C front
end for GCC as Free Software was something
of a PR coup for the Free Software Foundation.
Unfortunately, it was not so good from the
perspective of long-term cross-platform support.
The code that NeXT released was terrible and,
for the last ten years, has been largely ignored
by the GCC team. This improved slightly with
GCC 4.6, but still lags the current version of
Objective-C by about five years.

GCC has moderately good support for NeXT-
era Objective-C, and also supports the newer
exception-handling keywords. The GNUstep
project provides implementations of the Foundation
and AppKit frameworks that are the core of
NeXT and Mac development.

In 2007, Apple began work on a new compiler.
Clang is a front end for the *Low Level Virtual
Machine (LLVM)*, for C-family languages: C,
Objective-C, and C++. It is much more modular
than GCC, and is designed to be used for code
completion, syntax highlighting, and static
analysis as well as just compilation. Clang has
clean separation between the code used in the
different layers and isolates the runtime-specific
code into separate classes.

The compiler is only half of an Objective-C
implementation. The other half is the runtime
library. The GNU runtime was developed with
GCC and did not implement the functions

required for Objective-C 2. To remedy this, I wrote a framework as part of Étoilé that implemented most of the missing functionality and implemented the public runtime APIs that Apple introduced with OS X 10.5.

This framework is now part of GNUstep, for use with old versions of the GCC runtime. I've also written a new runtime, supporting the old GCC ABI and a new non-fragile ABI, which now has feature parity with OS X. This is developed as part of the GNUstep project and is referred to as either the *GNUstep runtime* or *libobjc2*.

With Clang, and the runtime provided by the GNUstep project, you get full support for all Objective-C 2 features, including non-fragile instance variables. This means that you can use Objective-C 2 on Windows, Linux, *BSD, Solaris, and so on. At least one person has been testing it on QNX, and it may also work on Symbian.

If you use the GCC version of the runtime, along with the Objective-C 2 framework in GNUstep, then you get some things, such as fast enumeration and declared properties, but you do not get any of the benefits of the new ABI. GCC 4.6 and later also ship with an updated runtime that provides the same level of compatibility, but without the need for the Objective-C 2 compatibility framework.

Compiling Objective-C Programs

```
0   $ gcc scanner.m
1   Undefined symbols:
2     "_OBJC_CLASS_$_NSAutoreleasePool", referenced
          from:
3         __objc_classrefs__DATA@0 in ccoRpaJq.o
4     "_objc_msgSend", referenced from:
5         _main in ccoRpaJq.o
6   ...
7   $ # On OS X
8   $ gcc -framework Foundation scanner.m
9   $ # On other platforms
10  $ gcc `gnustep-config --objc-flags --base-libs`
          scanner.m
```

The Clang front end is intended as a drop-in
replacement for GCC, so anywhere you see gcc
in some instructions, you can substitute clang.
On OS X, GCC is installed in /usr/bin/gcc, so it
is on your path. With slightly older versions
of the XCode tools, Clang was installed in
/Developer/usr/bin/clang, so you may need to
either specify the full path or add this location
to your path. On other platforms you will
generally find both on your path, if they are
installed.

If you are familiar with compiling C or C++
with either of these compilers, you will find
compiling Objective-C very familiar. If you just
specify a source file on the command line, the
compiler will attempt to compile and link it as
an executable.

Note: Apple's presentation at their 2011 developers' conference stated "GCC is going away." Apple no longer actively develops GCC and so it lacks support for more recently added language features and probably won't be shipped with a future version of Apple's developer tools.

Apple marketing is somewhat confusing when it comes to compilers. OS X 10.7 shipped with something that they described as Apple's LLVM Compiler 3.0. This is a snapshot of Clang from about half way between the 2.9 and 3.0 releases. If you run clang –version, you will see something like "based on LLVM 3.0svn" in the output.

Most of the time, this will not work. Objective-C programs require some other libraries. On OS X, the compiler drivers support an extra option; -framework, which specifies a framework bundle containing headers and a shared library. This is both a linker and preprocessor option.

The examples in this book all use the Foundation framework. On other platforms, this is typically implemented by the GNUstep Base library. These platforms typically don't support the -framework option. The gnustep-config tool provides an alternative. This will print the compiler options needed for compiling Objective-C and for linking against the base (Foundation) or gui (AppKit) libraries.

As with C and C++, you can specify -c to just

compile the file but not link and −o to specify the name of the output. If you are compiling more than one file, you probably want to use something a bit more advanced than running the compiler from the command line.

On OS X, you will probably use the XCode IDE. This lets you create projects with a number of different template types. If you need to compile these on other platforms, you can find a tool in the GNUstep repository called **pbxbuild**, which will compile them.

If you are working on some other platform, you can use GNUstep Make to build. This also works on OS X, so whichever option you choose, you should not have portability problems caused by your build system.

An Objective-C Primer

Objective-C is a very small set of additions to C. The first version of Smalltalk was created as a bet that it was possible to specify an entire general-purpose language on a single piece of paper. The Objective-C extensions to C are slightly more complicated than Smalltalk, but not by much.

If you already know C, then learning the Objective-C language will take an afternoon—less if you already understand Smalltalk-style object orientation. That's slightly misleading, of course. If learning Objective-C was really that simple, you'd feel a bit ripped off buying a book about it. Like Smalltalk, much of the reason that the Objective-C language is so simple is that it delegates a lot to the library.

The standard library for the original StepStone version of Objective-C was very small. It was intended to be used with C libraries, rather than as a standalone language. Now, most Objective-C code uses something based on the NeXT Foundation framework—either Apple's Foundation or the GNUstep Base library— as a standard library. This provides things like reference-counted memory management, standard data structures, forwarding mechanisms, and so on.

Much of what you would think of as part of the Objective-C language is really provided by the Foundation framework. It is possible to use Objective-C without Foundation, but it's the sort of thing people do to prove that they can, not because it's actually an intelligent thing to do.

Declaring Objective-C Types

```
6    NSMutableArray *mutableArray = [NSMutableArray
         new];
7    NSArray *array = mutableArray;
8    NSObject *object = array;
9    id obj = mutableArray;
10   mutableArray = (NSMutableArray*)object;
11   mutableArray = obj;
```

From: cast.m

Objective-C, as its name implies, adds objects to C. Specifically, objects following the Smalltalk model, which are instances of classes. Objects are always allocated on the heap and so are always referenced by pointer.

In the first implementations of Objective-C, which produced pure C from Objective-C, classes were turned into structure definitions describing the layout of the objects. You can still see some legacy of this in GCC error messages, which will occasionally refer to objects as "structures."

In C, you need an explicit cast to turn any structure pointer into any other kind of structure pointer. This rule is relaxed slightly for Objective-C. The layout of any object is defined by the *instance variables (ivars)* in the root class, then by the instance variables in each subsequent class down the hierarchy. Subclasses can only add new instance variables, not remove or rearrange ones from the superclasses. This means that it is always safe, in terms of memory layout, to cast a pointer to an instance of one class to a pointer to an instance of a superclass. It is also safe from the perspective of the object-oriented type system; any subclass will always respond to all of the messages that the superclass responds to.

Object pointers in Objective-C are identified by the name of the class, followed by a star, just as structure pointers are in C, although without the **struct** keyword. You can always cast a pointer to an instance of one class to a pointer to an instance of its superclass implicitly. This works even for indirect superclasses. For example, NSMutableArray is a subclass of

NSArray, which is a subclass of NSObject. You can cast an NSMutableArray to an NSArray or to an NSObject. Casting in the opposite direction, however, requires an explicit cast.

Objective-C also introduces a new pointer type: **id**. This is roughly analogous to **void**∗, when it comes to casting rules. You may cast any object pointer to **id** and you may cast **id** to any object pointer type, implicitly.

If you are used to an untyped language, such as Smalltalk, Ruby, or Python, then it can be tempting to use the **id** type exclusively. This is mostly safe, although there is one exception. Objective-C uses the name of a message for lookup, and does not include any type information. This means that you can declare two different methods (on different classes) with the same name but different types. When the compiler is generating a message send, it uses the type of the receiver to determine types of the arguments. This, in turn, defines the layout of the call frame. When there is only one method advertised anywhere with that name, the type information is not required. Static typing is also required if you want to access instance variables from outside an object, but doing this is generally considered bad style.

Although specifying static type information is not required, it is often a good idea. Aside from the one case just mentioned, it will not affect code generation, but it is used by the semantic analysis phase of the compiler. This can help catch some errors at compile time. For example, if you try adding an object to an NSArray instance, the compiler will warn you that the receiver does not respond to the relevant message. This lets you check whether you really meant NSMutableArray, or if you need to make a mutable copy of the array.

Note: In C++, it is common to use the **const** keyword to describe objects as immutable. In Objective-C, **const** is effectively useless. It specifies that the instance variables of an object may not be modified directly, but this is rarely done. It does not alter the messages that can be sent to an object, so an object that is declared as **const** remains mutable.
Most of the time when the distinction between mutable and immutable instances is required, Objective-C programmers use the *mutable subclass pattern*, where an immutable class has a mutable subclass. You can cast the mutable version to the immutable version implicitly, but you cannot make an immutable instance mutable.

The **Class** type is similar to **id**, but it may refer to classes. In Objective-C, a class is an object, so you can always use **id** instead of **Class**, just as you can use **id** instead of a specific object type.

Two other types are defined in the standard

Objective-C headers.[1] The **SEL** type is used
for selectors, which we'll look at later in this
chapter.

The last one is **IMP**, which stands for *Instance
Method Pointer*. This type refers to a pointer
to an Objective-C method. Most of the time,
you won't need to use this type at all. It is only
used for some of the very dynamic features of
Objective-C, and for optimization. We'll look at
some places where you might use it in Chapter
19.

Sending Messages

```
9    [anObject autorelease];
10   [anObject addObject: anotherObject];
11   [anObject setObject: anotherObject
12             forKey: aThirdObject];
```

From: exampleMessages.m

The most important addition to C that Objective-
C makes is sending messages. A message, as
I said in the last chapter, is a high-level flow
control construct.

This is the bit of Objective-C that tends to
intimidate people coming from languages such
as C++ and Java, because the syntax is taken
straight from Smalltalk and looks quite alien
to people more familiar with C syntax. This is

---

[1]If you are compiling with Clang, most of these types
have built-in definitions, so the headers are optional.

intentional. There is nothing in C that behaves the same way as an Objective-C message send, so having new syntax highlights the fact that you also have new semantics. Remember that Tom Love described it has a hybrid language, with a clear syntax separation between the pure C parts and "object land," which has Smalltalk-like syntax to accompany Smalltalk-like semantics.

The simplest kind of message send takes no arguments. An example of this might be the `-count` message sent to an array. Note the minus sign before the message name. This is the convention used in Objective-C documentation to indicate a message that is sent to an instance. A plus sign is used to indicate a message sent to a class, such as `+new` or `+arrayWithObject:`.

```
size = [anArray count];
```

This snippet gets the number of elements in an array and stores it in the variable **size**. In a language such as C++ or Java, the equivalent would be something like this:

```
size = anArray.size();
```

This same syntax in Objective-C would be used if **anArray** were a C structure and the **size** field were a function pointer. Because this means something very different to sending a message to an object, the designers thought it would be confusing to use the same syntax.

Messages that take one argument look very

similar. If you wanted to add an object to an Objective-C array, you'd use something like this:

```
[anArray addObject: anObject];
```

Things start to become a bit different when messages have more than one argument. As with Smalltalk, every argument has a separate name, so you'd insert the object at a specific index, like this:

```
[anArray insertObject: anObject
          atIndex: anIndex];
```

This makes Objective-C code very easy to read when you understand the basic syntax, because every message tells you what each argument is for. If you came across this message in documentation, it would be written like this: -insertObject:atIndex:. You can see from the two colons that it takes two arguments and from the text before the two colons what those arguments should be. As before, the minus sign indicates that this is a message sent to an instance.

If you send a message to an object that doesn't have a method to implement it, then a number of fallback methods are used. In the default implementation, the last of these will throw an exception (which you can catch at run time and work around). You can also ask an object before you send a message whether it knows how to handle it. We'll take a look at how to do this in Chapter 19.

Note: If you send a message to `nil`, a constant defined as (**id**)0, you do not get an error. Instead, you get a 0 value returned. This is very useful because you can send a string of messages to the result of previous message sends, and if one of them returns `nil` in the middle, then the rest will still work. This eliminates the need for a lot of tests for NULL in Objective-C code.

The behavior of sending a message that returns a structure to `nil` is undefined. If you do this in code compiled with GCC on SPARC, your program will crash with an illegal instruction signal. On OS X, the structure will be filled with random values, just like an uninitialized structure on the stack. You should always be careful to check that an object is not `nil` before sending it a message that returns a structure.

In Objective-C, like Smalltalk, classes are objects too. You can send them messages, just as you would send an object a message. You use the class's name as the receiver when you do this. The most common reason to send a message to a class is to create an instance of that class. Classes are responsible for creating their own instances in Objective-C. There is no equivalent of the **new** keyword in C++ or Java. The closest equivalent is the **+new** message, which you can send to a class. For example, you might create a new mutable array like this:

```
id anArray = [NSMutableArray new];
```

Although this looks quite similar, the language makes no guarantees about what this message will do. Some classes may create instances of a subclass, and some may return a singleton instance. It's only by convention that this gives you a new instance of the receiver.

The latest version of Objective-C introduces the concept of *method families*. These are implicit contracts that certain methods are expected to follow. For example, the **+new** method is expected to return an *owning reference* to an instance of the receiver. In the snippet above, the compiler would expect this to return a mutable array. If you tried to assign it to an NSMutableDictionary variable, for example, then it would generate a warning.

Understanding Selectors

```
5   SEL new = @selector(new);
6   SEL set =
7       @selector(setObject:forKey:);
```

From: selector.m

In C, you refer to functions by name. A function name can also be used as a pointer to that function. When you compile C code to assembly, the function becomes a label, which can be reached via a call instruction or instruction sequence.

Flow control in Objective-C is more dynamic.
You can take a pointer to a method, but most
of the time you want to send a specific message
to an object, rather than call a specific method.
If you call a specific method, you have to make
absolutely certain that the receiver really is the
class that you expect.

In C, you will often use function pointers
as arguments to other functions. The called
function will then call the one that is passed to
it. A common example of this is the `qsort()`
function in the C standard library. This sorts
an array, using a function to define the ordering
between the items.

In an Objective-C version, you might want to
compare objects by sending them a `-compare:`
message, rather than by using a function pointer.
Ideally, then, you'd want to pass the name of the
message to send in to the method implementing
the sort.

The name of a message is referred to as the
selector. This is an abstract representation of the
message name, and it has the **SEL** type, which is
an opaque type. You can create a selector with
the **@selector()** directive. This takes a constant
string representation of a message name and
turns it into a selector for that message name.

You can use selectors to call a method by name,
as we'll see in Chapter 19. A number of methods
in the Foundation framework take selectors as

Note: One of the major differences between the Apple and GNU implementations of Objective-C is that the GNU implementation uses *typed selectors*. Selectors are the names used to look up methods in a message send. In GNU Objective-C, they also include the encoding of the argument types of the message. This allows functions to check that they were called with the right argument types, which is very useful for distributed objects and a few other things.

The GNUstep runtime now uses type-dependent dispatch by default, meaning that the method lookup depends on the type encoding of the selector. Sending a message with a type signature that does not match the receiver is undefined behavior, so both the GNUstep runtime's approach of logging a warning or throwing an exception, and the Apple runtime's approach of corrupting the stack, are equally valid.

---

arguments. These are used in much the same way as C functions that take function pointers as arguments, for delayed execution, callbacks, sorting collections, and so on.

Declaring Classes

```objc
@interface Integer : NSObject
{
    int integer;
}
- (int)intValue;
- (void)addInteger: (Integer*)other;
@end
@implementation Integer
- (int)intValue { return integer; }
- (void)addInteger: (Integer*)other
{
    integer += [other intValue];
}
@end
```

From: integer.m

When you create a new class, you need to do two things: describe its public interface and write its private implementation. You will need three Objective-C keywords: **@interface**, **@implementation**, and **@end**.

Note that all new Objective-C keywords start with an @ sign. This is because this symbol is not allowed in C identifiers. Contrast this with C ǀ ǀ, which introduces identifiers such as **class**, which breaks any C code that uses **class** as a variable name.

Objective-C inherits the C compilation model, where the compiler expects a single file and separation is accomplished by making the preprocessor combine various files. By convention, interfaces to Objective-C classes are put in header files, with a .h extension, and implementations go in .m files. No one can remember why .m was chosen. The Objective-C designers have suggested that it might stand for "module," "methods," or "messages."

Because header files are inserted into the compilation unit by the preprocessor, before the Objective-C compiler sees them, this separation is not enforced. The same is true of C++ and opaque data types in C.

One slightly surprising aspect of Objective-C is that instance variables (what Java and C++ call "fields") are declared as part of the interface, not the implementation. This is an artifact of how early versions of Objective-C were implemented. Every object was converted to a C structure whose first field was a pointer to the class. To generate this structure, the compiler needed to be able to see all of the instance variables for all superclasses. One unfortunate side effect of this approach was that modifying the layout of a class meant that you had to recompile all of its subclasses.

Now, with the non-fragile ABI, you can hide private instance variables from the subclasses. Every reference to them goes via an indirection layer. The offset is now a variable, not a compile-time constant. New compilers allow you to define instance variables in **@implementation** contexts, as well as **@interface**s.

By default, Objective-C instance variables are

protected, meaning that they are only accessible by the class or its subclasses. If you prefix them with **@private** they are only available to the class, and with **@public** they are accessible anywhere. This is quite uncommon. There is little run-time checking of the access, and there are a few mechanisms for bypassing the access controls, so it's common to leave everything protected, only making instance variables public in private classes.

Note: Apple's non-fragile ABI restricts the visibility of ivar offset variables, creating a hard error if you try to access a private instance variable from a different compilation unit. It is still possible to access private instance variables by using runtime introspection and this protection is not available with other runtimes.

The basic structure of a class interface contains three parts. First is the definition of the place of the new class in the hierarchy:

@interface ClassName : Superclass <protocols>

The name of the class immediately follows the **@interface** keyword. Next there is a colon, and then the name of the superclass. It is possible to design new root classes, but it is quite complex to do correctly, so most of the time you will just use **NSObject** or **NSProxy** as your superclass.

After that, you may optionally specify a list

Note: With recent compiler versions, you
can prefix a class interface declaration with
__attribute__((weak_import)). This makes
all references to it weak. If you send a message to
the class and it is not linked, then this is equivalent
to sending a message to nil. Subclasses of a class
imported in this way will not be resolved until the
superclass is loaded. This lets you define a class
that inherits from a class in an optionally loaded
bundle.

---

of protocols, separated by commas, in angle
brackets. Protocols in Objective-C are like
interfaces in Java. They define lists of methods
that the object must implement.

Next comes the list of instance variables. This
follows the same syntax as defining a structure
in C. A simple class definition with just instance
variables and no methods would look like this:

```
@interface NoMethods : NSObject
{
  int integer;
  NSObject *object;
  float floatingPoint;
}
@end
```

Anything that is valid in a C structure definition
is valid here. If you are using Objective-C++,
you may also add pointers to C++ objects and
C++ objects that have a trivial constructor.

Finally, you list the public methods that the
class implements. Rather than making some
up for this, let's look at some real method
declarations:

```
+ (id)new;
- (void)appendString: (NSString*)aString;
```

The plus sign in front of the first method
declaration indicates that this is a method
attached to the class. You can send a +new
message to the class and it will give you an
object pointer back. The **id** type is a new type
introduced with Objective-C, roughly similar to
the **void*** type in C, but restricted to pointing
to Objective-C objects.

Note that the return type and the types of the
parameters use the same syntax as type casts.
This highlights another important difference
between message sends and C function calls.
The method is compiled to a function and
called via a pointer that is looked up at run
time. When you send a message, the compiler
is implicitly casting the method pointer to a
function described by these types. This syntax
is also intended to emphasize that the argument
does not have to be an **NSString***; it just has to
be something that you can cast to an **NSString***.

The implementation part of the class
definition is much simpler. This starts with
the **@implementation** directive and contains
definitions of all of the class's methods, like this:

@implementation NewClass

```
+ (int)classVersion
{
  return 2;
}
- (void)log
{
  fprintf(stderr, "log message received");
}
@end
```

One important point to note is that you do not have to declare all of the methods that a class implements. Methods that are not declared in the class interface are considered to be private. Calling them will generate a compile-time warning, and a future version of the class may stop responding to them altogether.

Using Protocols

Like classes, protocols in Objective-C are objects. The behavior of protocols was one of the things that Apple changed with the modern runtime. Previously, protocols were identified by name, and two protocols were considered equivalent if they had the same name. This meant that if you had two protocols with the same name declared in different libraries, you couldn't tell which of them an object implemented. More importantly, you couldn't look up a protocol and see what methods it required.

With Objective-C 2, protocols are now unique.

You can now get a protocol by name and inspect it. This sometimes worked with the old model, but it depended on whether the compiler had already emitted a full definition of it.

You can get a reference to a protocol with the **@protocol()** keyword. The main reason for doing this is to test protocol conformance.

```
if (![delegate conformsToProtocol: @protocol(
    DelegateProtocol)])
{
  testIndividualMethods = NO;
}
```

You might use something like this snippet in a method that sets a delegate. If the delegate conforms to the protocol, it is guaranteed to implement all of the methods in that protocol, so you don't need to test each one. If it doesn't, you may need to test each message before you send it.

Protocols give you both compile-time and run-time type checking. You can require an object to conform to a protocol by putting the name in angle brackets after the type name. Here are some examples:

```
id <NSCopying> a;
id <NSObject,NSCopying> b;
NSObject<NSCopying> *c;
```

Here, you can assign any object that implements the NSCopying protocol to a. Objects assigned to b must also implement the NSObject protocol,

which any object that inherits from **NSObject** or
NSProxy will automatically. Finally, **c** must be
a subclass of **NSObject** and must implement the
NSCopying protocol.

The compiler will generate a warning—not an
error—if you assign an object to a variable that
requires it to conform to a protocol that is not
in the list that it is declared as conforming
to. This is not a hard error because it may
still implement all of the methods required by
the protocol, even though it doesn't advertise
protocol conformance.

Adding Methods to a Class

```
3   @interface NSObject (Logging)
4   - (void)log;
5   @end
6   @implementation NSObject (Logging)
7   - (void)log
8   {
9     NSLog(@"%@", self);
10  }
11  @end
```

From: logging.m

One of the biggest differences between Objective-
C and a language such as C++ or Java is
the idea of *categories*. These were present in
Smalltalk, but as a way of grouping methods
together for documentation. In Objective-C,
they allow you to add methods to a class, even

if you don't have access to the source code.

Category definitions are similar in structure to class definitions. A category cannot change the instance variables of a class, nor its superclass, so these parts of the **@interface** directive are omitted. A category name is added in brackets after the class name. In the preceding code, you can see a simple category interface and implementation that adds a −log method to NSObject. You can then send a −log message to any object and have it dumped to the console.

Note that both the interface and implementation of the category are optional. In the next section, we'll look at why specifying a category interface without a corresponding implementation can be useful. Specifying an implementation without an interface is useful if you want to just *replace methods* in an object.

Methods declared in a category will replace methods of the same name declared in the class. This ordering is guaranteed, so if there is a conflict, the category will always take precedence. If there are two categories that define the same method, the one that is used is undefined.

One of the less-documented features of categories is that they let you add protocol conformance to a class. In the Foundation framework, the various collections have no common superclass and do not implement a common protocol. In the EtoileFoundation framework, we add

categories to them all, making them adopt the
ETCollection protocol. This lets us use this
protocol in places where we need some collection,
but don't care exactly which type.

```
3   @protocol Collection
4   - (BOOL)isEmpty;
5   @end
6   @interface NSArray (Collection) <Collection> @end
7   @interface NSSet (Collection) <Collection> @end
8   @implementation NSArray (Collection)
9   - (BOOL)isEmpty
10  {
11    return [self count] == 0;
12  }
13  @end
14  @implementation NSSet (Collection)
15  - (BOOL)isEmpty
16  {
17    return [self count] == 0;
18  }
19  @end
```

From: collection.m

The collection.m example shows a (very)
simplified version of this. The Collection
protocol is added to both the NSSet
and NSArray classes. If you send a
-conformsToProtocol: message to an
instance of either of these classes, with
@protocol(Collection) as the argument, it will
return **YES**.

There is a special case for categories, where you
declare a category interface with no name. This

is referred to as a *class extension*. Unlike other categories, which should be accompanied by a separate **@implementation** directive specifying the category name, methods declared in class extensions are expected to appear in the main **@implementation** directive for the class. You can use this for forward-declaring private methods.

With the most recent Objective-C compilers, you may also declare instance variables inside class extensions. You can also declare instance variables inside **@implementation** contexts, just as you do inside **@interface** contexts. These two mechanisms allow you to move implementation details out of public headers.

If you are declaring private instance variables, then you should declare them in the **@implementation** context. This ensures that nothing that shouldn't access them will do so by accident. If you are declaring public or protected instance variables that should only be accessed within the same library, then you should declare them in a class extension in a private header. In new code, you should only declare instance variables that are expected to be directly accessed by users of your code in public headers.

Using Informal Protocols

```
3   @interface NSObject (InformalProtocol)
4   - (id)doSomething;
5   @end
6   // Objective-C 2 only:
7   @protocol InformalProtocol
8   @optional
9   - (id)doSomething;
10  @end
```

From: informalProtocol.m

Quite often, you want to define a set of methods that you'd like a class to implement, but that are optional. This is particularly common for delegates, where you will test whether the delegate implements a given method before sending it a message.

With Objective-C 2, protocols can contain methods that are declared as optional, but prior to that it was common to implement informal protocols using categories. If you create an interface for a category on **NSObject** but don't provide an interface definition for it, then the compiler will assume that every **NSObject** subclass responds to the messages declared in the interface and therefore won't generate a warning when you send any of them to an object.

Of course, not every object really will implement these methods, so you need to make sure you use **-respondsToSelector:** to test whether an object really does, before you send the message.

Synthesizing Methods with Declared Properties

```
3  @interface Integer : NSObject
4  @property (nonatomic,assign) int integer;
5  @end
6  @implementation Integer
7  @synthesize integer;
8  @end
```

From: synth.m

One of the big additions to Objective-C 2 was *declared properties*. These let you define some aspects of the semantics of an accessor and then synthesize the relevant methods if you don't need any special handling.

Note: The dot syntax is one of the most controversial changes that Apple has made to Objective-C. It violates one of the core principles of Objective-C—that new semantics should always use new syntax—by reusing the structure field accessor syntax for message sending. The dot syntax is also useful for hiding bad design; it encourages indirect references, which violate the Law of Demeter.

Properties also introduce some new syntax. They are implemented in terms of message sends. The example at the start of this chapter will create both -integer and -setInteger: methods. You can call these just as you would any other methods, but you can also use the dot notation, like this:

```
obj.integer = 12;
int i = obj.integer;
obj.integer += 42;
```

The last case is the most useful. Expanding this to the traditional Objective-C message syntax would look like so:

```
[obj setInteger: [obj integer] + 42];
```

It's worth remembering that both of these will generate precisely the same code. The first looks more efficient, but it is not. In both cases, you have two message sends and one addition. This is significantly more expensive than if **obj** were a C structure.

Note: The term "property" is used in Smalltalk documentation to refer to any instance variable that can be manipulated via accessors. It is used in slightly older Objective-C documentation in the same way. Specifying *declared* properties, rather than just properties, helps reduce this ambiguity.

A property declaration contains two parts: an interface and an implementation. The interface defines the name and type of the property, as you'd expect, but it also defines some high-level semantics.

Properties are atomic by default. This incurs some overhead, so you probably want to specify nonatomic in most properties that you create. Atomicity of accessor methods does not make an object thread-safe, and you are almost always better off using some higher-level locking for sharing objects between a thread.

Consider the nonatomic.m example. This declares an atomic property. You then use a single increment operation in the code. You'd expect this to be an atomic increment, but it isn't. This single statement expands to two message sends with an increment in between them.

```
3   @interface NotReallyAtomic : NSObject
4   @property  int a;
5   @end
6
7   int add(NotReallyAtomic *obj)
8   {
9     obj.a += 1;
10  }
```

From: nonatomic.m

All that atomic means, in the context of properties, is that both the set and get methods will try to acquire the same lock, when not using garbage collection, so the object will not be accidentally deallocated if you try setting it in one thread and getting it in the other thread. In garbage collected mode, and for non-object properties, the *nonatomic* has no meaning.

Properties can be either **readwrite** or **readonly**,

indicating whether assigning to them is supported. If you define a `readwrite` property and are not using garbage collection, you also need to define the setter's semantics.

Note: Sometimes, you will want to have a read-write property, but only make it readable in the public interface. Class extensions provide a mechanism for doing this. If you declare the property read-only in the main interface, but then redeclare it read-write in the class extension, an **@synthesize** directive in the main **@implementation** will create the setter and getter. However, attempts to use the setter anywhere that the class extension is not visible will create a compiler error.

There are several options for setter behavior. The simplest—and the only option for non-object types—is `assign`. This sets the value by trivial assignment. For non-object types, this just copies the value. For objects, things are a bit more complicated.

The exact semantics of the various property accessors change depending on the memory management mode. With reference counting (manual or automatic), `assign` performs simple assignment when you set the value. When you access the value, it will return the pointer for nonatomic properties, or retain then autorelease it for atomic ones.

The next option, `retain`, only makes sense in reference counting modes. When setting a `retain` property, the new value is retained and the old value released. In garbage collected mode, both `assign` and `retain` are equivalent.

A `copy` property is similar to a `retain` property. When setting it, the new value is sent a `-copy` message instead of `-retain`. You should commonly use this for properties that have immutable types. For example, if you declare an `NSString*` property, then using `copy` ensures that you will have an immutable string, even if someone sets it with an `NSMutableString*` instance. Immutable objects return themselves from `-copy`, so this will only create a copy if one is actually required to ensure that the property is not accidentally mutated.

If you use automatic reference counting or garbage collection, which we'll look at in detail in Chapter 3, Memory Management, then you can use `weak`. A `weak` property does not prevent its value from being deleted and will set it to `nil` when all other references have gone.

Modern compilers also support `unsafe_unretained` as a property type. This is equivalent to `assign`, but is more explicit about the lack of safety.

The property types that only make sense for objects may also be used for C pointer types that are declared with `__attribute__((NSObject))`. This attribute tells the compiler that the C type is really an Objective-C object. Core Foundation objects and blocks (see the "Using Blocks" section) are common examples of this. They are exposed in headers that may be included in C programs, so they do not explicitly expose Objective-C types, but they may be used as Objective-C objects in Objective-C.

Once you have declared a property interface, you must provide an implementation. Properties are just a way of defining accessor methods. The property `a` in the last example is implemented with `-a` and `-setA:` methods. The first returns the value of the property, and the second sets it to a new value.

You can implement these methods yourself. You might also inherit them from a superclass. If this is the case, the compiler might not be able to see them and will generate a warning. You can suppress this by providing an `@dynamic` line for the property. This tells the compiler that the methods do really exist and will be resolved at run time.

Alternatively, you can use **@synthesize** to tell the compiler to generate the accessor methods for you. Synthesized property methods refer to the instance variable with the same name as the property. These methods call a runtime library function with the offset of the instance variable and some flags indicating the kind of property.

In general, you should try to always use

@synthesize. The compiler will then generate a method with the correct semantics for your current compilation mode. This lets you switch between manual reference counting, automatic reference counting, and garbage collection easily. You won't need to modify any accessor methods; the compiler will do it for you.

With older Objective-C ABIs, instance variables all needed to be declared in the **@interface** description so that the compiler could turn them into C structures. With a non-fragile ABI, this is not the case. The @synthesized directive can create new instance variables that are not part of the class's public interface.

Understanding self, _cmd, super

```
8  id method(id self, SEL _cmd, ...);
```

From: object.m

Every Objective-C method is compiled to a function. This has two hidden arguments: **self** and **_cmd**. The first of these is quite obvious: It's the receiver of the message. If it's an instance message **self** will be an instance of the class. If it's a class message, it will be the class itself.

In C++, the **this** keyword is almost equivalent to **self** in Objective-C, but with one crucial difference: **self** is not a keyword. It is the name of an argument. Assigning to **this** in C++ will cause an error. Assigning to **self** in Objective-C is permitted.

The second hidden argument is the *selector* for the message. This is required for things such as forwarding to work correctly. When you send a message to an object that the object doesn't know how to handle, it will construct an **NSInvocation** object encapsulating the message and then pass it to –forwardInvocation:.

Because neither of these hidden arguments are keywords, you may use them both outside of methods as identifiers, although the C specification reserves identifiers that start with an underscore for the implementation, so it is probably best not to use **_cmd**. The normal scoping rules apply, so you can also declare a variable called **self** inside of a method and have it hide the version that was passed as a parameter. The compiler will generate a warning if you do this, because it's a stupid thing to do, but it is semantically valid.

The **super** pseudo-variable is a bit more complicated. This is only valid when used as the receiver of a message. It will generate a message send where **self** is the receiver but where the method is looked up in the superclass, not the current class. This is how you call methods that you have overridden.

Sending messages to **super** uses a different method lookup function that takes a pointer to an **objc_super** structure as the argument. This structure contains both the target class and the target object.

The superclass is fixed at compile time. When you compile an Objective-C class, all messages to **super** will be looked up on the class that is defined as the superclass in the class interface.

For most code, this doesn't matter, but it's something that you need to remember if you are using the runtime library functions to add methods to a class. If the method you are attaching to a new class sends messages to **super**, it will send them to the wrong class.

It's also worth noting that message sends to the superclass are implemented differently in categories with the GNU runtime. The class implementation context is in the same compilation unit as the class structure, because the class structure is generated by the compiler from the code contained in the **@implementation** context. The superclass pointer can be found just by looking this up and getting the superclass field.

In a category, the class structure is not available. It must be looked up at run time. This makes superclass messages slower when sent from methods defined in categories. The Apple runtimes work around this by making the linker resolve the external class reference.

The reason for the dynamic lookup is to support class posing, a technique where one class replaces the definition of another at run time. With the

Modern Apple runtime, class posing is no longer supported. Every class exports its structure as a public symbol, so the linker will resolve the class pointers at load time.

The interaction between class posing and categories is subtly different between the legacy Apple runtime and the GNU runtimes, but you can avoid worrying about this by simply avoiding using class posing. This is a good idea anyway. There are lots of corner cases where posing doesn't behave quite as you might expect, and it's very easy to use it to write code that works fine for you but doesn't work on an almost identical machine.

Understanding the isa Pointer

```
1   typedef struct objc_object *id;
2
3   struct objc_object
4   {
5     id isa;
6   };
```

From: object.m

In C++, classes are structures. You can subclass a C structure as a C++ class. When you call a method on a C++ class, you are really calling a C function with a mangled name and a pointer to the structure as the first (hidden) argument.

In Objective-C, structures and classes are very different. Before the introduction of non-fragile

ABIs, you could use the **@defs** keyword in a
structure definition to create a structure with
the same layout as a class, but you could not use
classes and structures interchangeably.

The difference between an object and a structure
is that you can send a message to a class. This
works because the first instance variable in a
structure is a pointer to the class structure. This
instance variable is, by convention, called **isa**, as
in "this object is a. . . ." If you define a new root
class, you must remember to add this instance
variable.

As with the **self** and **_cmd** hidden arguments,
the **isa** pointer is just another instance variable;
it is not a keyword. Contrast this with calling
a virtual method in C++. A C++ object
that has virtual methods contains a (hidden)
pointer to a vtable. This is a simple array of
function pointers. When you call the method,
the compiler dereferences the vtable pointer and
calls the function at the correct offset.

You cannot use the vtable to find anything out
about the object, and its layout is part of the
target platform's ABI definition, not part of the
language. The **isa** pointer is very different. It is
an explicit instance variable, and therefore it's
accessible just like any other instance variable. It
points to a **Class**, which is a **typedef** provided
by the Objective-C runtime headers[2] and defined

---

[2]Clang treats it as a built-in type if a definition is not
provided.

as either an opaque type or a pointer to a public C structure, depending on the runtime.

On runtimes where the exact layout of the class structure is private, you will still find functions for inspecting it. These can tell you the offsets of instance variables, the names and type signatures of methods and properties, the superclass, and so on.

You can look at the `isa` pointer on other objects. The **id** type is defined as a C structure (with no access control) containing just the pointer to the class, so you can read it just as you would any other field in a structure.

In the latest version of Objective-C, directly accessing the `isa` pointer is deprecated. You should use the `object_getClass()` and `object_setClass()` functions instead.

The latest runtimes borrow a trick from Smalltalk and hide very small objects inside a pointer. Objects are always word-aligned, so the low few bits of a pointer will always be 0. This lets you do things like store 31-bit integer in a 32-bit pointer, with the lowest bit set to 1 to differentiate it from a real object. Treating such a value as a pointer and trying to access the `isa` pointer directly would break things quite badly.

Objective-C objects may forward messages, and the object pointer that you have might be a proxy. If you want to get another object's class, you should send it a `-class` message instead. This is slower, but it won't break in the presence of proxies.

You can test whether an object is a proxy by sending it an −isProxy message, but if you're sending one message anyway, you may as well just send one to get the class.

Initializing Classes

```
4  @implementation Init
5  + (void)load
6  {
7    NSLog(@"+load called");
8  }
9  + (void)initialize
10 {
11   NSLog(@"+initialize called");
12 }
13 - (id)init
14 {
15   NSLog(@"-init called");
16   return self;
17 }
18 @end
19
20 int main(void)
21 {
22   [NSAutoreleasePool new];
23   NSLog(@"main() entered");
24   id init = [[Init alloc] init];
25   init = [[Init alloc] init];
26   return 0;
27 }
```

From: classInit.m

In C++, you can perform static initialization

by assigning the result of a function to a global or static variable. In C, you can use extensions such as GCC's __attribute__((constructor)) to achieve the same result. These both cause a particular function to be called before the main() function.

It's difficult to use these correctly. The order in which they are called is undefined. Objective-C has an equivalent. The +load method on a class is called when the class is registered with the runtime, before the main() function.

It is not safe to send arbitrary messages from this method. The class itself, all of its superclasses, and the constant string class are all guaranteed to have been loaded. Other classes might have been, but this is not guaranteed, and even if it works for you, it might not work if the load order changes slightly.

A safer alternative is the +initialize method. This is called automatically, by the runtime, when the first message is sent to the class. Typically, the first message will be something like +alloc, to create an instance of the class, but it might be something requesting the class name or a singleton instance.

The +initialize method lets you perform lazy initialization of things the class needs. This won't be called before the main() function, so everything will be loaded already and the process will be in a well-defined state.

If you implement both of these methods, you

can see the order of execution. First the +load
method is called, as soon as the class is loaded.
When the run-time loader finishes, it calls the
main() function. When you send a message to
the class, the +initialize method is called,
then the method you actually called, and then
you can send an −init message to the returned
instance.

```
1   a.out[2690:903] +load called
2   a.out[2690:903] main() entered
3   a.out[2690:903] +initialize called
4   a.out[2690:903] -init called
5   a.out[2690:903] -init called
```

Output from: classInit

Note that the +initialize method is only
called once. The second time you send a
message to the class, it is delivered directly. The
+initialize method call is also thread-safe. If
you send two messages to the same class at the
same time from different threads, one will block
until the other finishes running the +initialize
method, and then both will continue.

Reading Type Encodings

```
3   typedef struct _s
4   {
5     int i;
6     float f;
7     NSArray *a;
8     char *str;
9     unsigned short shorts[5];
10  } s;
11
12  int main(void)
13  {
14    const char *encoding = @encode(s);
15    printf("Encoding: %s\n", encoding);
16    return 0;
17  }
```

From: type.m

Much of Objective-C depends on run-time introspection. Objective-C objects can be introspected by sending the messages, but this is not the case for C types. To help with this, Objective-C defines a way of encoding C types as strings. Each of the primitive types is encoded as a single character. For example, **int** encodes as *"i"*, whereas **unsigned long long** encodes as *"Q"*. The convention of uppercase letters representing the unsigned version and lowercase letters representing the signed version is applied across all of the integers.

These type encodings can include arbitrarily complex C types, as you can see from the output of the type.m example.

```
1    Encoding: {_s=if@*[5S]}
```

Output from: type

This example gives the type encoding of a
structure that contains primitive C types,
an Objective-C object, and a C array. The
type encoding is generated by the compiler, in
response to the **@encode()** directive, which is
used in a similar way to **sizeof()**, taking a type
as an argument and returning a type encoding.

The structure itself is represented by a pair of
braces. Inside this is the name of the structure,
followed by an equals sign and then the type
encodings of each of the elements.

The next four characters show the type
encodings of the first four fields. There are two
things to note here. The first is that Objective-
C objects are all encoded as *"@"*, irrespective of
their static type information. The second is that
char* is encoded as *. All other pointers are
encoded as ^ followed by the pointee type, but C
strings get special treatment.

The remainder of this encoding is the array.
This is in square brackets, with the number
of elements followed by the type of a single
element.

Objective-C type encodings crop up anywhere
you do any kind of introspection on the level
of C types. If you ask for the types of a

method or an instance variable, you will get
the type encoding. This is very useful. In the
EtoileSerialize framework, I use this information
to iterate over the type encodings of instance
variables and automatically serialize them.

Using Blocks

```
3   int(^getCounter(void))(void)
4   {
5     __block int counter;
6     int(^block)(void) =
7       ^(void) { return counter++; };
8     return Block_copy(block);
9   }
10
11  int main(void)
12  {
13    [NSAutoreleasePool new];
14    int(^block)(void) = getCounter();
15    block(); block();
16    NSCAssert(block() == 2,
17        @"Block counted incorrectly");
18    int(^block2)(void) = getCounter();
19    block2(); block2();
20    NSCAssert(block2() == 2,
21        @"Block didn't start from 0");
22    return 0;
```

From: block.m

With 10.6, Apple introduced *blocks* to the C
language. Although these are a C language
extension, they are most often used in
conjunction with Objective-C.

Blocks are *closures*, sometimes called lambdas.

The name comes from Smalltalk, where the
`BlockClosure` class encapsulates closures. The
syntax for creating blocks is quite ugly. It is
based on the C syntax for function pointers, but
with a caret replacing the asterisk.

Blocks can be used almost exactly like function
pointers. You can call them just like functions,
but you can't cast them to function pointers
because they have a different calling convention.
Just like methods, a block has a hidden
argument.

In the example, the `getCounter()` function
returns a new block that implements a counter.
Every time you call this block, it returns a value
one greater than the last time you called it. This
works because the `counter` variable in the scope
where the block was created is declared with the
`__block` specifier.

Any variables on the stack that blocks reference
will be copied to the heap and reference counted.
When you call `Block_copy()`, the block itself
is copied to the heap if it's on the stack, or
has its reference count incremented if it is not.
`Block_copy()` is actually a macro that wraps
the `_Block_copy()` function and casts the return
type from **void**∗ to the type of the argument.

Each block returned by the `getCounter()`
function in the example has a copy of the
`counter` variable, because it is an automatic
(stack) variable, and so subsequent calls to the
function are creating a new version.

In the latest version of the Foundation framework, you will find a lot of methods that take blocks as arguments. You can, for example, iterate over an array with a block as an argument.

Blocks don't add any expressiveness to the C language. A block is just a function pointer and a data pointer hidden inside a single structure, with some extra logic in the compiler to insert the data pointer as a hidden argument to the function when it is called.

This doesn't mean that blocks are not useful. After all, the same is true of Objective-C; it doesn't let you do anything that you can't do in C, it just adds some syntactic sugar that makes some things easier.

Like Objective-C objects, blocks have an `isa` pointer and can be sent messages. They are instances of the `NSBlock` private abstract class, which implements the `NSCopying` protocol.

Most of the object-like behavior of blocks is undocumented. You can store them in Objective-C collections, but don't depend on their ability to understand any specific messages. With the latest versions of Clang, blocks also support introspection, exposing their types as Objective-C type encodings.

We'll look at blocks in more detail in Chapter 15.

3

Memory Management

If you come from a C or C++ background, you're probably used to tracking ownership of objects and manually allocating and destroying them. If you're coming from a language such as Java, you're probably accustomed to having the garbage collector take care of all of this for you.

Objective-C does not, at the language level, provide anything for allocating or deallocating objects. This is left up to C code. You commonly allocate objects by sending their class a +alloc message. This then calls something like malloc() to allocate the space for the object. Sending a -dealloc message to the instance will then clean up its instance variables and delete it.

The Foundation framework adds reference counting to this simple manual memory management. This makes life much easier, once you understand how it works. Newer compilers provide some assistance for you, eliminating the need to write the reference counting code yourself.

Retaining and Releasing

```
6   NSArray *anArray = [NSArray array];
7   anArray = [[NSArray alloc] init];
8   [anArray release];
```

From: retainRelease.m

Every object that inherits from **NSObject** has a reference count associated with it. When this reference count reaches 0, it is destroyed. An object created with **+alloc** or any of the related methods, such as **+new** or **+allocWithZone:**, begins life with a reference count of one.

To control the reference count of an object, you send it **-retain** and **-release** messages. As their names would imply, you should use these messages when you want to retain a reference to an object, or when you want to release an existing reference. The **-retain** message increments the object's reference count, and the **-release** message decrements it.

You can also send a **-retainCount** message to an object to determine its current reference count. It's tempting to use this for optimization and invoke some special cases when you are sure there is only one reference to an object. This is a very bad idea. As the name implies, this method tells you the number of retained references to the object, not the number of references. It is common not to bother sending a **-retain** message to objects when you create a pointer to them on the stack. This means that an object may be referenced in two or more places, even though its retain count is only one.

Pointers in Objective-C are divided into two categories: *owning references* and *non-owning references*. An owning reference is one that contributes towards the retain count of an object. When you call a method like **+new** or **-retain**, you get an owning reference to a new object. Most other methods return a non-owning reference. Instance variables and global variables are typically owning pointers, so you should assign owning references to them. You also need to ensure that you delete the existing owning reference (by sending a **-release** message) when performing an assignment.

Temporary variables are typically non-owning references. Automatic reference counting and garbage collection, which we'll look at later in this chapter, both introduce special kinds of non-owning references.

Assigning to Instance Variables

```
26   - (void)setStringValue: (NSString*)aString
27   {
28     id tmp = [aString retain];
29     [string release];
30     string = tmp;
31   }
```

From: ivar.m

There are a few things that you have to be careful about when using reference counting in this way. Consider the following simple set method:

```
14   - (void)setStringValue: (NSString*)aString
15   {
16     [string release];
17     string = [aString retain];
18   }
```

From: ivar.m

This looks sensible. You release the reference to the old value, then retain the new value and assign it. Most of the time, this will work, but in a few cases it won't, and that can be confusing to debug.

What happens if the value of **aString** and **string** are the same? In this case, you are sending the same object a **-release** message then a **-retain** message. If some other code holds references to this object, it will still work, but if not then the first message will cause the object to be destroyed and the second will be sent to a dangling pointer.

A more correct implementation of this method would retain the new object first, as shown at the start of this section. Note that you should assign the result of the –retain message because some objects will return another object when you retain them. This is very rare, but it does happen on occasion.

Finally, this method is not thread-safe. If you want a thread-safe set method, you need to retain the new value, perform an atomic exchange operation on the result and the instance variable, and then release the old value. In general, however, it is almost impossible to reason about code that supports this kind of fine-grained concurrency, and the amount of cache churn it causes will offset any performance gains from parallelism, so it's a terrible idea. If you really need it, it's better to use declared properties to synthesize the accessor than try to write it yourself.

Automatic Reference Counting

With the release of iOS 5 and Mac OS X 10.7, Apple introduced *Automatic Reference Counting (ARC)*. Conceptually, you can think of this as having the compiler automatically figure out when –retain and –release should be called, and calling them for you. The implementation is somewhat more complicated.

Note: Most of the examples in this book use manual reference counting. This is intentional. Even though ARC is recommended for new development, there is a lot of legacy code around that does not use it. Even if you are using ARC, you should still understand the retain and release semantics that are implicitly added for you. It's very easy for a programmer who is comfortable with manual reference counting to switch to using ARC, just as it's useful to understand your CPU's instruction set even if you never write any assembly code.

Rather than inserting message sends directly into the code, the compiler front end inserts calls to functions like `objc_retain()` and `objc_release()`. The optimizer then tries to combine or eliminate these calls. In the simple case, these functions do the equivalent of a message send. In some common cases, they are significantly more efficient.

In simple use, you can forget about memory management when using ARC. If you are using a recent version of XCode, then ARC is the default. If you are compiling on the command line or with some other build system, add -fobjc-arc. Now just forget about retaining and releasing objects.

It would be nice if life were that simple. Unfortunately, ARC does have some limitations. More specifically, it formalizes the fuzzy boundary between C memory and Objective-C objects. ARC divides pointers into three categories. Strong pointers follow the same retain/release semantics that we've looked at already. Weak pointers, which we'll look at later, are non-owning references that are automatically zeroed when the object is destroyed. Unsafe unretained pointers are pointers that are ignored by ARC: You are responsible for tracking the lifetime of objects stored in them.

By default, all object pointers in instance variables or on the stack are strong. Object pointers in structures have no default. They must be explicitly marked with the `__unsafe_unretained` ownership qualifier. Even though this is the only permitted ownership for these pointers, it must be explicitly stated to provide a reminder to people reading the code that ARC will ignore it.

Returning Objects via Pointer Arguments

```
3    __weak id weak;
4    int writeBack(id *aValue)
5    {
6      *aValue = [NSObject new];
7      weak = *aValue;
8      return 0;
9    }
10
11   int main(void)
12   {
13     @autoreleasepool
14     {
15       id object;
16       writeBack(&object);
17       NSLog(@"Object: %@", object);
18       object = nil;
19       NSLog(@"Object: %@", weak);
20     }
21     NSLog(@"Object: %@", weak);
22     return 0;
23   }
```

From: writeback.m

In ARC mode, pointer-to-pointer arguments
are somewhat complicated. These are typically
used for two things, either passing arrays or
returning objects. If you are passing an array
down the stack, then you should make sure that
you declare it as **const**. This tells the compiler
that the callee will not perform any assignments
to it, so ARC can pass the array without any
complex interaction.

If you are returning an object via this mechanism, ARC produces some fairly complex code. In the example at the start of this section, the call to `writeBack()` generates code that is roughly equivalent to this:

```
id tmp = [object retain];
writeBack(&tmp);
[tmp retain];
[object release];
object = tmp;
```

In `writeBack()`, the new object will be autoreleased before storing it in the temporary value. This means that, at the end of this, `object` contains an owning reference to the new object.

If you declared `object` as `__autoreleasing id`, the generated code is a lot simpler. This will simply autorelease the value initially stored in `object`, which will have no effect because the initial value for all object pointers—even with automatic storage—is `nil`, and will pass the pointer directly and expect the callee to store a non-owning (autoreleased) pointer in it, if it modifies it.

When you run this example, you'll see that the weak reference is only zeroed when the autorelease pool is destroyed. The `writeBack()` function stores an autoreleased object into the passed pointer in all cases, and never releases the passed value. The caller is always responsible for ensuring that the value passed in is a non-owning reference, which it does either by ensuring that it's a pointer to an autoreleased object or a copy of a pointer to a retained object.

If you instead mark the parameter **out** (only allowed on method parameters, not C function parameters) then the callee guarantees that it will not read the value, so the compiler will skip the step where it makes a copy of the pointer in `object` before the call.

If you need to pass multiple objects up the stack, then you should probably return an `NSArray` instance. There are some alternatives, but they are sufficiently complex that it's simply not worth the effort: they're easy to get subtly wrong and spend ages debugging, and if you do manage to get it right, you'll probably find it's slower than using an `NSArray`.

If you are passing multiple values down the stack, then you should declare an array type with an explicit ownership qualifier for the parameter, not a pointer type. For example, `__unsafe_unretained id[]` instead of `id*`. This ensures that the writeback mechanism is not used.

Avoiding Retain Cycles

```
19   - (void)setDelegate: (id)aDelegate
20   {
21     delegate = aDelegate;
22   }
```

From: ivar.m

The problem with pure reference counting is that
it doesn't detect cycles. If you have two objects
that retain references to each other, then neither
will ever be freed.

In general, this is not a major problem.
Objective-C data structures tend to be acyclic,
but there are some common cases where
cycles are inevitable. The most common is the
delegation pattern. In this pattern, an object
typically implements some mechanisms and
delegates policy to another object. Most of
AppKit works in this way.

The delegate needs a reference to the object, and
the object needs a reference to its delegate. This
immediately creates a cycle. The common idiom
that addresses this problem is that objects do
not retain their delegates. If you pass an object
as an argument to a -setDelegate: method,
you need to make sure that some other object
holds a reference to it, or it will be deleted
prematurely.

With ARC, you have two choices: You can
either mark the instance variable as **__weak**

or as `__unsafe_unretained`. The former is
safer, because it ensures that there is no chance
of a dangling pointer: When the delegate is
destroyed, the instance variable will be set to
`nil`.

There are two disadvantages of using a weak
pointer. The first is portability. Weak pointers
work on iOS 5, Mac OS X 10.7, and with
GNUstep, but they don't work on older versions
of iOS or Mac OS X. The other disadvantage
is performance. Every access to a weak pointer
goes via a helper function. This checks that the
object was not in the process of deallocation and
retains it if it is still valid, or returns `nil` if it is
not.

In contrast, unsafe unretained pointers are
just plain pointers. They are cheap to access
and work on any deployment target. Their
disadvantage is that you are responsible for
ensuring that you don't try to access them after
the pointee has been deallocated.

A good compromise is to use weak pointers
when debugging and unsafe unretained pointers
for deployment. Add debug assert statements
checking that the pointer is not `nil` before you
send it any messages, and you'll end up with a
helpful error, rather than a crash, if you have
bugs.

Migrating to ARC

If you are starting a new project in XCode, ARC
will be the default and there is little reason
not to use it. If you are working on an existing
code base, then you are probably using manual
reference counting. You can save some long-term
development effort by moving to ARC, but it is
a little bit more involved than simply flipping a
compiler switch.

Clang provides a migration tool that will
attempt to rewrite Objective-C code to use
ARC. This can be invoked from the command
line via the -ccc-arcmt-check and -ccc-arcmt-
modify arguments. The first reports any things
in the code that cannot be automatically
translated. The second actually performs the
rewriting—modifying the original file—if there
are no errors.

For simple Objective-C code, the migration tool
will just work. The most obvious thing that
it does is remove all **-retain**, **-release**, and
autorelease message sends. It will also remove
the explicit [**super** dealloc] from a **-dealloc**
method: That call is now inserted automatically
by the compiler. ARC automatically releases
all instance variables, so you will only need to
implement **-dealloc** at all if you are freeing
malloc()'d memory or similar.

If you implement custom reference counting
methods, then you will need to delete them. A
common reason for this is to prevent accidental

> **Note:**   ARC actually creates a -.cxx_destruct method to handle freeing instance variables. This method was originally created for calling C++ destructors automatically when an object was destroyed. The visible difference of this with ARC is that Objective-C instance variables are now deallocated after -dealloc in the root class has finished, not before. In most cases, this should make no difference.

deallocation of singletons. This is less important with ARC, because programmer error is less likely to cause an object to be prematurely deleted.

The biggest problems come if you are trying to store Objective-C pointers in C structures. The simplest solution is just not to do that: Use Objective-C objects with public instance variables instead. This lets the compiler handle memory management for the object, as well as the fields.

The only time when using structures referring to Objective-C objects is considered safe is when you are passing them down the stack. The object pointers can then be __unsafe_unretained qualified without any problems, as long as they remain valid in the caller.

You will notice that you no longer have any assign properties after using the migration tool. These will be rewritten as unsafe_unretained or **weak**, depending on whether the deployment target that you've selected supports weak references. You may want to explicitly change some to `unsafe_unretained` if they are used for breaking simple cycles and you find weak references to be a performance problem.

The migration tool will try to insert `__bridge` casts where required, but these are worth checking. These casts are used to move objects in and out of ARC-managed code. In non-ARC Objective-C, you are free to do things like (**void***)someObject, because object pointers are just C pointers that you can send messages to. In ARC mode, this cast would be ambiguous because the compiler doesn't know what the ownership semantics of **void*** are supposed to be, so it is rejected.

The migration tool will rewrite this as (`__bridge` **void***)someObject, but that may not be what you want. We'll look at these casts in more detail in the "Interoperating with C" section.

Autorelease Pools

```
3   id returnObject(void)
4   {
5     return [[NSObject new] autorelease];
6   }
7
8   int main(void)
9   {
10    @autorelease {
11      id object = returnObject();
12      [object retain];
13    }
14    // Object becomes invalid here.
15    [object release];
16    return 0;
17  }
```

From: autorelease.m

Aside from cycles, the biggest problem with reference counting is that there are short periods when no object really owns a particular reference. In C, deciding whether the caller or callee is responsible for allocating memory is a problem.

In something like the **sprintf()** function, the caller allocates the space. Unfortunately, the caller doesn't actually know how much space is needed, so the **snprintf()** variant was added to let the callee know how much space is available. This can still cause problems, so the **asprintf()** version was added to let the callee allocate the space.

If the callee is allocating the space, who

is responsible for freeing it? The caller, presumably, but because the caller didn't create it, anything that checks for balanced `malloc()` and `free()` calls will fail to spot the leak.

In Objective-C, this problem is even more common. Lots of methods may return temporary objects. If you're returning a temporary object, it needs to be freed, but if you're returning a pointer to an instance variable, it doesn't. You could retain such a pointer first, but then you need to remember to release every single object that is returned from a method. This quickly gets tiresome.

The solution to this problem is the *autorelease pool*. When you send an object an `-autorelease` message, it is added to the currently active `NSAutoreleasePool` instance. When this instance is destroyed, every object added to it is sent a `-release` message.

The `-autorelease` message is a deferred `-release` message. You send it to an object when you no longer need a reference to it but something else might.

If you are using `NSRunLoop`, an autorelease pool will be created at the start of every run loop iteration and destroyed at the end. This means that no temporary objects will be destroyed until the end of the current iteration. If you are doing something that creates a lot of temporary objects, you may wish to create a new autorelease pool, like so:

```
id pool = [NSAutoreleasePool new];
[anObject doSomethingThatCreatesObjects];
[pool drain];
```

Note that you send an autorelease pool a -drain
message rather than a release message when
you destroy it. That is because the Objective-
C runtime will ignore -release messages when
you are in garbage collected mode. The -drain
message in this mode provides a hint to the
collector, but does not destroy the pool, when
you are in garbage collected mode.

In OS X 10.7, Apple made autorelease
pools part of the language. Programs that
explicitly reference the NSAutoreleasePool
class are considered invalid in ARC mode
and the compiler will reject them. The
replacement is the @autoreleasepool construct.
This defines a region where an autorelease
pool is valid. In non-ARC mode, this will
insert exactly the same code as the above
snippet. In ARC mode, it inserts calls to
the objc_autoreleasePoolPush() and
objc_autoreleasePoolPop() functions, which
do something similar.

Using Autoreleased Constructors

```
4   + (id)object
5   {
6     return [[[self alloc] init] autorelease];
7   }
```

From: namedConstructor.m

I said in the last section that objects created with +alloc have a retain count of one. In fact, all objects are created with a retain count of one, but objects created with a named constructor, such as +stringWithFormat: or +array, are also autoreleased.

If you create an object with one of these mechanisms, you must send it a -retain message if you want to keep it. If you don't, it will be collected later when the autorelease pool is destroyed.

This is a convention that is important to observe in your own classes. If someone creates an instance of one of your classes with a named constructor, he will expect not to have to release it. A typical named constructor would look something like the one at the start of this section.

Note that, because this is a class method, the **self** object will be the class. By sending the +alloc message to **self** rather than to the class name, this method can work with subclasses automatically.

With ARC, these conventions are formalized
in *method families*. Methods that begin **alloc**,
new, **copy**, or **mutableCopy** return an *owning*
reference, a reference that must be released if
not stored. Other methods return a non-owning
reference, one that has either been autoreleased
or is stored somewhere else with a guarantee
that it will not be released.

Autoreleasing Objects in Accessors

```
34   - (NSString*)stringValue
35   {
36     return [[string retain] autorelease];
37   }
```

From: ivar.m

Another common issue with reference counting,
as implemented in Foundation, is that you
commonly don't retain objects that you only
reference on the stack. Imagine that you have
some code like this:

```
NSString *oldString = [anObject stringValue];
[anObject setStringValue: newString];
```

If the **-setStringValue:** method is implemented
as I suggested earlier, this code will crash
because the object referenced by **oldString**
will be deleted when you set the new string
value. This is a problem. There are two possible

solutions, both involving autorelease pools. One is to autorelease the old value when you set the new one. The other is the definition of the `-stringValue` method from the start of this section.

This ensures that the string will not be accidentally destroyed as a result of anything that the object does. Another common idiom is to substitute a `-copy` message for `-retain`. This is useful if the instance variable might be mutable. If it's immutable, `-copy` will be equivalent to `-retain`. If it's mutable, the caller will get an object that won't change as a result of other messages sent to the object.

Supporting Automatic Garbage Collection

```
o   $ gcc -c -framework Cocoa -fobjc-gc-only
        collected.m
1   $ gcc -c -framework Cocoa -fobjc-gc collected.m
```

Starting with OS X 10.5, Apple introduced automatic garbage collection to Objective-C. This can make life easier for programmers, but in most cases it comes with a performance penalty. Apple's collector uses a lot of memory to track live references and therefore is not available on the iPhone. It is also not supported with older versions of OS X and has only limited support with GNUstep, so you should avoid using garbage collection if you want to write portable code.

If you compile your code in garbage collected mode, all -`retain`, -`release`, and -`autorelease` messages will be ignored. The compiler will automatically insert calls to functions in the runtime for every assign operation to memory on the heap.

Code must be compiled with garbage collection support to use the garbage collector. This will insert calls to a set of functions that, on the Mac runtime, are declared in objc-auto.h on any assignment to memory on the heap.

These functions make sure that the garbage collector is aware of the write. These are required because the collector is concurrent. It will run in a background thread and will delete objects when it can no longer find references to them. The collector must be notified of updated pointers, or it might accidentally delete an object that you have just created a reference to.

You have two options when compiling for garbage collection. If you compile with the -fobjc-gc-only flag your code will only support garbage collection. If you compile with the -fobjc-gc flag, the code will support both reference counting and automatic garbage collection. This is useful when you are compiling a framework. You must still remember to add -`retain` and -`release` calls in the correct

```
110  OBJC_EXPORT BOOL objc_atomicCompareAndSwapGlobal(
         id predicate, id replacement, volatile id *
         objectLocation)
111      __OSX_AVAILABLE_STARTING(__MAC_10_6,
             __IPHONE_NA) OBJC_ARC_UNAVAILABLE;
112  OBJC_EXPORT BOOL
         objc_atomicCompareAndSwapGlobalBarrier(id
         predicate, id replacement, volatile id *
         objectLocation)
113      __OSX_AVAILABLE_STARTING(__MAC_10_6,
             __IPHONE_NA) OBJC_ARC_UNAVAILABLE;
114  // atomic update of an instance variable
115  OBJC_EXPORT BOOL
         objc_atomicCompareAndSwapInstanceVariable(id
          predicate, id replacement, volatile id *
          objectLocation)
116      __OSX_AVAILABLE_STARTING(__MAC_10_6,
             __IPHONE_NA) OBJC_ARC_UNAVAILABLE;
117  OBJC_EXPORT BOOL
         objc_atomicCompareAndSwapInstanceVariableBarrier
         (id predicate, id replacement, volatile id *
         objectLocation)
```

From: objc-auto.h

places, but users of your framework can then use it with or without collection.

Interoperating with C

In garbage collected mode, not all memory is scanned. Anything allocated by `malloc()` is invisible to the garbage collector. If you pass an object pointer as a **void*** parameter to a C function, which then stores it in `malloc()`'d memory, it becomes invisible to the collector and may be freed even though there are still references to it.

In ARC mode, the compiler will handle pointers that are on the stack or in instance variables for you automatically, but it won't track pointers in structures or anything else explicitly declared as __unsafe_unretained.

Normally, you would send a -retain message to an object before storing it on the heap, but that does nothing in garbage collected mode and is forbidden in ARC mode. Instead, you have to use the CFRetain() function. This will increment the object's reference count, irrespective of whether the collector is running. The collector will only free objects when their retain count is zero and it cannot find any references to them in traced memory.

When you have finished with a reference that is outside of the collector's scope, you need to call CFRelease().

ARC provides a richer memory model for this kind of operation. Explicit casts from object to non-object pointer types are no longer allowed. They must be replaced by *bridged casts*. Consider the following bit of code in non-ARC mode:

```
void *aPointer = (void*)someObject;
```

In ARC mode, this would create an untracked pointer from a tracked pointer, which is not

something that you want to do without thinking.
You have three basic options. The first is
most commonly used for on-stack variables, or
variables pointing to objects that are guaranteed
to be referenced elsewhere:

```
void *aPointer = (__bridge void*)someObject;
```

This performs the cast with no transfer of
ownership. If all other references to someObject
are dropped, then aPointer becomes a dangling
pointer. If the **void*** pointer is going on the
heap somewhere and should keep an owning
reference to the object, then you should use a
retained bridging cast:

```
void *aPointer = (__bridge_retained void*)
    someObject;
```

This will move a single owning reference
out of ARC's control. This is roughly
equivalent to sending a **-retain** message to
someObject before it is stored. If you write
(__bridge_retained **void***)someObject with
no assignment, then this tells the compiler to
retain the object. Doing this is considered very
bad style. You should use the inverse operation
when casting back to an object pointer:

```
id anotherObjectPointer = (__bridge_transfer
    id)aPointer;
aPointer = NULL;
```

This transfers an owning reference into ARC's
control. ARC is now responsible for releasing the

object, so it is important to remember to zero the C pointer. If you are not taking ownership of the pointer, then you should use a simple __bridge cast.

Understanding Object Destruction

```objc
3   @interface Example : NSObject
4   {
5     void *cPointer;
6     id objectPointer;
7   }
8   @end
9   @implementation Example
10  - (void)finalize
11  {
12    if (NULL != cPointer) { free(cPointer); }
13    [super finalize];
14  }
15  - (void)dealloc
16  {
17    if (NULL != cPointer) { free(cPointer); }
18  #if !__has_feature(objc_arc)
19    [objectPointer release];
20    [super dealloc];
21  #endif
22  }
23  @end
```

From: dealloc.m

There are three methods that are invoked during the destruction of an object, depending on the mode. One will run every time, but cannot be written by you. The -.cxx_destruct method

is always called by the Objective-C runtime and
handles the destruction of any fields that the
compiler is responsible for cleaning up. This
includes C++ objects in Objective-C++ mode
and Objective-C object pointers in ARC mode.

The other two methods are `-finalize` and
`-dealloc`. In garbage collected mode, you do
not need to do anything to relinquish references
to Objective-C objects, but you do still need to
clean up any resources that are not managed
by the garbage collector. This includes closing
file handles, freeing memory allocated with
`malloc()`, and so on. If your class has instance
variables that need this kind of manual cleanup,
then you should declare a `-finalize` method.

Note: The garbage collector will typically call
`-finalize` methods in a special cleanup thread.
This means that `-finalize` methods must be
thread safe. If they refer to global resources, then
they must ensure that doing so does not introduce
race conditions.

If you are not using garbage collection, then you
should do cleanup in a `-dealloc` method. The
contents of this method depend on whether or
not you are using ARC. Traditionally, `-dealloc`
methods were full of `-release` message sends to
every instance variable that the class declared.
With ARC, this is not required. ARC will
relinquish any owning references to objects in

-.cxx_destruct, so you only need to clean up non-object instance variables in –dealloc.

In both GC and manual retain/release mode, you should forward the message to the superclass, calling [**super** dealloc] or [**super** finalize] as appropriate. In ARC mode, explicitly calling –**dealloc** is not permitted. Instead, ARC will insert a [**super** dealloc] call at the end of your –**dealloc** method in any non-root class.

Note that the example at the start of this section is overly complicated. In real code, you are unlikely to need to support both ARC and manual retain/release modes. Both can interoperate in the same program. The only reason to support non-ARC mode is if you wish to support legacy compilers.

Using Weak References

```
4   __weak id weak;
5
6   int main(void)
7   {
8     id obj = [NSObject new];
9     weak = obj;
10    obj = nil;
11    objc_collect(OBJC_FULL_COLLECTION);
12    fprintf(stderr, "Weak reference: %p\n", weak);
13    return 0;
14  }
```

From: weak.m

One of the nicest things about Apple's garbage collection implementation is the existence of *zeroing weak references*. Pointers that are not retained are often referred to as "weak" in Objective-C documentation that predates the garbage collector. These are references that are allowed to persist beyond the lifetime of the object. Unfortunately, there is no automatic way of telling whether they are still valid.

Weak references were found to be so useful with the garbage collector that they are now also supported by ARC, with slightly different semantics. The ARC implementation provided for backwards compatibility does not support weak references, so they can only be used with ARC on Apple platforms if you restrict yourself to OS X 10.7 or iOS 5 and later.

Note: Weak references in a reference counted environment, such as those referencing delegates, are commonly used to eliminate retain cycles. This is not needed in a tracing environment, so you can use strong references for pointers to delegates and anywhere else you might have a retain cycle.

If you declare an object pointer **__weak**, you get a zeroing weak reference. This is not counted by the garbage collector when determining if an object is still live and does not increment the object's reference count when assigned to in ARC mode. If all of the references to an object are weak, it can be destroyed. Afterwards, reading the weak references will return `nil`.

Weak references are most commonly used in connection with things such as notifications. You will keep a weak reference to an object and keep sending it messages as long as it is referenced elsewhere, then you can have it cleaned up automatically later.

Cocoa now comes with some collections that let you store weak references. Older versions of the Foundation framework provide `NSMapTable` and `NSHashTable` as opaque C types, with a set of C functions to use them. These interfaces are still available, but with 10.5, Apple made these two C types into classes.

The `NSMapTable` type is a general form of `NSDictionary` that can be used to store any pointer-sized types as both values and keys. With garbage collection, you can use this class to store mappings to and from strong or weak object pointers as well. This is useful for things such as `NSNotificationCenter`, so that objects can be collected while they are still registered to receive notifications and can be automatically removed from the notification center when this happens.

The example at the start of this section shows an important difference between ARC and GC modes. If you compile and run this example with garbage collection enabled, you will probably see it print an object address. This is because the garbage collector will still see stale temporaries while scanning the stack.

In contrast, this will always print 0 in ARC mode. ARC, unlike GC, is entirely deterministic. Assigning **nil** to the strong pointer decrements the object's reference count and triggers deallocation. The weak pointer is zeroed before deallocation begins and so is guaranteed to be zero by the time the **fprintf()** is reached.

Allocating Scanned Memory

```
15    id *buffer =
16       NSAllocateCollectable(
17          10 * sizeof(id),
18          NSScannedOption);
```

From: gc.m

If you allocate memory with **malloc()**, it is invisible to the garbage collector. This is a problem if you want, for example, something like a C array containing objects. We've already looked at one solution to this. You can call **CFRetain()** on the object you are about to store and **CFRelease()** on the old value, and then swap them over.

This is not ideal, although it will work. The other option is to allocate a region of memory from the garbage collector. The **NSAllocateCollectable()** function is similar to **malloc()**, but with two important differences.

The first is that the memory that it returns is garbage collected. There is no corresponding `NSFreeCollectable()` function. When the last pointer to the buffer disappears, the buffer will be collected.

Note: The Apple collector does not support interior references, so you must make sure you keep a pointer to the start of the region. Pointers to somewhere in the middle of the buffer will not prevent it from being freed.

The second difference is that the second parameter to this function defines the kind of memory that you want. If you are going to be using the buffer for storing C types, you can just pass zero here. If you pass `NSScannedOption`, the returned buffer will be scanned as a possible location of object pointers, as well as pointers to other memory regions returned by `NSAllocateCollectable()`.

4

Common Objective-C Patterns

Every programming language encourages a different set of design patterns. Understanding the common ones used throughout the Foundation framework makes understanding the framework as a whole, and writing Objective-C code, a lot easier.

This chapter provide an overview of some of the most common patterns in Objective-C. If you want to read more, you can find a much more detailed overview in *Cocoa Design Patterns*, by Erik M. Buck and Donald A. Yacktman (Addison-Wesley, 2009).

Supporting Two-Stage Creation

```
6    NSMutableString *buffer =
7      [[NSMutableString alloc] init];
8    NSMutableArray *array =
9      [[NSMutableArray alloc]
10        initWithObject: buffer];
```

From: allocInit.m

One of the patterns you've probably already seen is the *two-stage creation pattern.* In traditional, pre-NeXT, Objective-C, you create an object by sending the class a +new message. When you implemented a new class, you would override +new to call the superclass implementation and then perform that class's initialization.

NeXT changed this, splitting object creation and object initialization into two different methods. The +new method still works, but now it sends a +alloc message to the class and a -init message to the returned object.

The +alloc method itself, by default, calls +allocWithZone:. This takes an NSZone as an argument. This is an opaque type encapsulating an allocation zone. This was used very heavily on NeXT systems, to make efficient use of the very small amount of memory that these machines came with. It does not work particularly well on OS X, and is not properly supported by all classes, so it's something of a vestigial feature in a lot of modern Objective-C code.

When you create a new class, you override the
−init method, or provide a new designated
initializer.

Note: You can still find some evidence of the
old-style creation in GCC. When +new was used to
create objects, it was common to create the new
instance and then assign it to **self** in the class
method. There is some code in GCC to support
this, allowing instance variable access from class
methods. This feature was deprecated a long time
ago, so you now get a warning when you try it.

It is very rare to override +alloc. Occasionally,
people do this to implement per-class pools or
enforce singletons, but it's quite unusual. If you
are implementing a singleton class, you may
override +alloc to return an existing instance
if one exists. We'll look at that later in this
chapter.

Copying Objects

```
3   @interface Pair : NSObject <NSCopying>
4   @property (nonatomic, retain) id first, second;
5   @end
6   @implementation Pair
7   @synthesize first, second;
8   - (id)copyWithZone: (NSZone*)aZone
9   {
10    Pair *new = [self->isa allocWithZone: aZone];
11    new.first = first;
12    new.second = second;
13    return new;
14  }
15  @end
```

From: copy.m

The Foundation framework includes a function
called NSCopyObject(). You might logically
expect that this will copy an object, and you'd
be almost right. It creates a new object with
the same class as the original and then uses
something like memcpy() to copy the instance
variables over.

This works fine for objects that only have
primitive C types as their instance variables, but
not so well for others. Object pointers need to be
sent a –retain message when they are copied.
C pointers may need some other things done
to them, particularly if they are opaque types
returned from some other library.

Without information about exactly what the
relationship between objects is, the copy function

cannot create a true copy automatically. Some objects should not even support copying. What, for example, would you expect the semantics of copying an object that encapsulates a socket to be? Would you get two objects encapsulating the same socket?

The only thing that really knows how to make a copy of an object is the object itself. If the object implements the NSCopying protocol, you can send it a -copyWithZone: message to get the copy. This takes an NSZone as the argument.

Most code these days doesn't bother with NSZone. NSObject provides a -copy method, which just calls -copyWithZone: with the default zone as the argument. Although you may always call -copy, you should implement -copyWithZone:.

This method normally begins by sending an +allocWithZone: message to the receiver's isa pointer, which creates a new instance. It may then call an initializer, or it might fill in the instance variables itself.

Note: If you are inheriting from a superclass that implements the NSCopying protocol, you should send a -copyWithZone: message to **super** in your -copyWithZone: implementation and then only copy the instance variables your subclass added.

An object returned by -copy (or

-copyWithZone:) should be treated in the
same way as one returned by +alloc (or
+allocWithZone:). Its initial retain count will
be one, so you must remember to send it a
-release or -autorelease message at some
point, to avoid memory leaks.

Archiving Objects

```
55  void roundTripWithArchiver(id object, Class coder
        , Class decoder)
56  {
57    NSData *data = [coder
          archivedDataWithRootObject: object];
58    id copy = [decoder unarchiveObjectWithData:
          data];
59    NSCAssert(data, @"Archiving failed");
60    NSCAssert(copy, @"Unarchiving failed");
61    NSCAssert(([object integer] == [copy integer]),
62      @"Integer wasn't copied correctly");
63    NSCAssert([[object string] isEqual: [copy
          string]],
64      @"String wasn't copied correctly");
65  }
```

From: archive.m

Often, you need some parts of your program's
state to persist for longer than a single
invocation. You can store some pure-data object
types in *property lists*, as we'll see in Chapter 7,
but what about storing arbitrary objects?

You can write data out in some custom (or
public) format and then re-create the objects

from this. Defining new file formats just because you want a few objects to persist is a bit more effort than most programmers want to exert, however.

Fortunately, Foundation provides the answer in the **NSCoding** protocol. This defines two methods: **-initWithCoder:** and **-encodeWithCoder:**. A lot of the standard classes implement this protocol, and it's relatively easy to implement yourself.

The object passed as an argument to these methods is a coder. This is a class that encapsulates some data representation. On older systems, this was typically **NSArchiver**, but on newer ones it will usually be **NSKeyedArchiver**. The older **NSArchiver** interface just let you write a stream of (typed) values. Keyed archives, however, support storing something more like a dictionary. They let you store key-value pairs and then read them back in a different order.

There are two parts to supporting archiving. Your object must be able to write itself to an archive, and it must be able to read itself back. In the **-encodeWithCoder:** method, you must write all of the object's state to the coder.

This does not necessarily mean all of the object's instance variables. Some objects have instance variables that are just used for caching information that can be reconstructed from elsewhere. It is generally better to reconstruct these after awaking than to store them.

```objc
34   - (void)encodeWithCoder: (NSCoder*)aCoder
35   {
36     if ([aCoder allowsKeyedCoding])
37     {
38       [aCoder encodeInt: integer
39                  forKey: @"integer"];
40       [aCoder encodeObject: string
41                     forKey: @"string"];
42     }
43     else
44     {
45       [aCoder encodeValueOfObjCType: @encode(int)
46                                  at: &integer];
47       [aCoder encodeObject: string];
48     }
49
50   }
```

From: archive.m

It's a good idea to support both keyed and non-keyed coders. Often, non-keyed archivers are used for transient encodings (for example, transmission over a network), whereas keyed coders are used for persistent data.

Keyed archivers have more convenient methods for archiving primitive C types. You can send things such as –encodeInt:forKey: messages. The older-style archivers only have one method for storing primitive C types, which takes the Objective-C type encoding and a pointer to the variable.

The corresponding method for loading can be a bit more complicated. The archiver stores the

```
12  - (id)initWithCoder: (NSCoder*)aCoder
13  {
14    if ([aCoder versionForClassName: [self
          className]] != 0)
15    {
16      [self release];
17      return nil;
18    }
19    if ([aCoder allowsKeyedCoding])
20    {
21      integer =
22        [aCoder decodeIntForKey: @"integer"];
23      string = [aCoder decodeObjectForKey: @"string
              "];
24    }
25    else
26    {
27      [aCoder decodeValueOfObjCType: @encode(int)
28                                  at: &integer];
29      string = [aCoder decodeObject];
30    }
31    string = [string retain];
32    return self;
33  }
```

From: archive.m

class version for every object that it stores. You should set this in +initialize by sending a +setVersion: message to **self** when you change an object's instance variable layout.

The -initWithCoder: method might need to load archives from older versions of your program, so it should check the version and handle the archive differently if it corresponds to an old version.

It's also important to remember to call the superclass implementation of both of these methods if, and only if, the superclass conforms to the **NSCoding** protocol. If it doesn't, but does have some state that you wish to persist, you are responsible for archiving this as well as your subclass's instance variables.

Creating Designated Initalizers

```
16   - (id)initWithSelectorName: (NSString*)aSel
17                    arguments: (NSArray*)args
18   {
19     if (nil == (self = [super init]))
20       { return nil; }
21     selector = [aSel copy];
22     arguments = [args mutableCopy];
23     return self;
24   }
25   - (id)initWithSelectorName:(NSString*)aSel
26   {
27     return
28       [self initWithSelectorName: aSel
29                        arguments: nil];
30   }
31   - (id)init
32   {
33     return [self initWithSelectorName: nil];
34   }
```

From: designatedInit.m

Most of the classes we've looked at so far have been initialized using the -init method. This method is the *designated initializer* in NSObject.

If you subclass NSObject, you will usually
override this method.

When a new NSObject subclass is created,
all of its instance variables are set to zero.
Your initializer may then set some of them to
something else, and acquire any other resources
that the object requires.

Note: The -init method in NSObject
does not do anything, it just returns **self**. This
means that it is tempting to avoid sending an
-init message to **super** in direct subclasses
of NSObject. This is generally considered bad
practice, because a category on NSObject might
replace this method with one that actually does
something.

Not all classes retain **-init** as their designated
initializer. By convention, the initializer that
takes the most arguments is the designated
initializer. All other initializer methods will call
this one.

This approach makes subclassing much easier.
A lot of classes provide a number of convenience
methods for initialization. If you had to override
all of these in every subclass, you would end up
with a lot of code that didn't add any value.

If the superclass uses the designated initializer
pattern, you only need to override one initializer.
The example in this section is taken from the
LKMessageSend class in LanguageKit. This

is an abstract syntax tree node representing a message send operation. The superclass's designated initializer is `-init`, so this class calls that from its own designated initializer. This class overrides `-init`, but the overridden version calls this class's designated initializer.

If you subclass this class, you just have to override the `-initWithSelectorName:arguments:` method, and you only need to do that if you add instance variables that need initialization. People sending a `-init` message to your class will get an initialized instance back.

Enforcing the Singleton Pattern

```objc
@implementation Singleton
static Singleton *sharedInstance;
+ (void)initialize
{
  if ([Singleton class] == self)
  {
    sharedInstance = [self new];
  }
}
+ (Singleton*)sharedInstance
{
  return sharedInstance;
}
+ (id)allocWithZone: (NSZone*)aZone
{
  if (sharedInstance &&
      [Singleton class] == self)
  {
    [NSException raise: NSGenericException
               format: @"May not create more than
                one instance of singleton."];
  }
  return [super allocWithZone: aZone];
}
@end
```

From: singleton.m

Singletons are the object-oriented version of global variables. A singleton class only has one instance. There are lots of these in Objective-C, but they all follow the same general pattern.

The example at the start of this section is a skeleton class that only permits a single instance of itself to be created. This follows the convention of returning the singleton instance in response to a +sharedInstance message. A lot of singleton classes put the class name in this message name, in place of Instance.

To get the shared application object in an AppKit application, for example, you will send a +sharedApplication message to NSApplication. This class is a special case of a singleton, because it stores its shared instance in the global NSApp variable. If the application has already started, you can use this variable directly, avoiding the message send to get the application object.

The most common mistake with singletons is to introduce a race condition in creation. This particular singleton is storing an instance of itself in a private variable. It it tempting to create this in the +sharedInstance method. That will work fine for single-threaded applications, but what about multithreaded ones?

If you send the +sharedInstance message simultaneously from two threads, what happens? Both might test the variable, find that it hasn't been created, and then create it. To get around this, you could use a lock.

A much simpler solution is to create the instance in the +initialize method. This method is called by the runtime the first time a message is sent to the class. It is the runtime's responsibility to ensure that this method completes before any messages are delivered to the class by other threads.[1]

Note: The Apple documentation recommends using **@synchronized(self)** in the +sharedInstance method for creating singletons. That approach is both significantly slower and requires more code than the approach proposed in this section, so it has little to recommend it.

You don't need to override **+allocWithZone:** in a singleton, but it provides a little bit extra runtime checking if you do. The sample code will throw an exception if you try to allocate a new instance of the class after the singleton instance has been created.

Note the tests in both the **+allocWithZone:** and **+initialize** methods. These are needed for subclassing. You don't want to throw an exception if someone creates a subclass of your singleton object. Subclassing singletons is quite tricky, so you may skip this extra test if you don't want to support it.

Delegation

Objective-C doesn't support multiple inheritance. This is not a huge limitation, because it's very hard to use multiple inheritance

---

[1]There is a long-standing bug in the GCC runtime that prevents this from working correctly, but it's fixed in the GNUstep runtime.

well, but with some problems it seems like the natural solution.

The idea behind the *delegation pattern* is similar to that behind inheritance and prototypes: You allow one object to define some subset of the behavior of another object.

You won't see this in the Foundation framework much, but it's very common in AppKit or UIKit code. Each user interface object uses delegation to allow you to define what happens in response to user interface events.

Several patterns are related to delegation, and they are all related to the general rule that you should favor object composition over inheritance. This is important for loose coupling, because it makes it much easier to reuse the code.

If you have a C++ class with three superclasses providing some aspects of its behavior, then it is a lot harder to modify than an Objective-C class delegating aspects of its functionality to three other classes.

Providing Façades

```objc
11  @interface Control : View
12  {
13    id cell;
14  }
15  @end
16  @implementation Control
17  - (id)selectedCell
18  {
19    return cell;
20  }
21  - (BOOL)isEnabled
22  {
23      return [[self selectedCell] isEnabled];
24  }
25  - (void)setEnabled: (BOOL)flag
26  {
27    [[self selectedCell] setEnabled: flag];
28    [self setNeedsDisplay: YES];
29  }
30  @end
```

From: facade.m

One very common use for delegation is the *façade pattern*. This wraps one or more private or semi-private objects in a public interface. This is very commonly used in Objective-C to provide something like multiple inheritance, where an object combines behavior from several distinct objects, delegating some of its functionality to each one.

The NSControl hierarchy in AppKit is a good example of this. Classes in this hierarchy inherit behavior from NSView and delegate behavior to an NSCell subclass. NSView provides features such as a graphics context, event handling, and interaction with the view hierarchy. The cell provides features such as drawing. The example at the top of this section is a (very) simplified version of **NSControl**.

When you click on a button in OS X, you are usually clicking on an instance of **NSButton**, which is an **NSControl** subclass using an **NSButtonCell** for its implementation. As a programmer, you can use controls almost interchangeably and you can also reuse the cells that they contain. If you see a button in a table or outline view, for example, this is drawn with an **NSButtonCell**, not with an **NSButton**.

In Chapter 19, we'll look at using the Objective-C forwarding mechanisms to quickly and easily implement this kind of façade. It's also possible—and common—to implement them simply by calling the methods in the wrapped object or objects directly.

This approach is much more flexible than multiple inheritance, because it allows the same class to be used with lots of different delegates. In C++, you would use template classes to achieve the same effect. These have different advantages. The Objective-C version generates a lot less code, which translates to better instruction cache usage. The C++ version makes certain categories of optimization (primarily inlining) easier at compile time.

Creating Class Clusters

```
26  static Pair *placeHolder;
27  + (void)initialize
28  {
29    if ([Pair class] == self)
30    {
31      placeHolder = [self alloc];
32    }
33  }
34  + (id)allocWithZone: (NSZone*)aZone
35  {
36    if ([Pair class] == self)
37    {
38      if (nil == placeHolder)
39      {
40        placeHolder =
41          [super allocWithZone: aZone];
42      }
43      return placeHolder;
44    }
45    return [super allocWithZone: aZone];
46  }
47  - (Pair*)initWithFloat: (float)a float: (float)b
48  {
49    return [[FloatPair alloc] initWithFloat: a
            float: b];
50  }
51  - (Pair*)initWithInt: (int)a int: (int)b
52  {
53    return [[IntPair alloc] initWithInt: a int: b];
54  }
```

From: classCluster.m

Class clusters are very common in Objective-C.
A lot of the Foundation classes are class clusters,
and you may find it useful to implement some
more of your own.

A class cluster is an *abstract superclass* that hides concrete subclasses. This is easier in Objective-C than many other languages, because there is no keyword for object creation. When you send a message to a class asking for a new instance, the class may return an instance of itself, but it may also return an instance of some subclass.

If you create an **NSArray** using **+arrayWithObjects:**, you may get a subclass that wraps a simple C array. If you create one using **+arrayWithArray:**, you are likely to get one that just references the other array.

Another good example is **NSNumber**. This wraps a single C primitive value. You could implement this with two instance variables: a union of all of the possible value types and another saying which one it is. This would waste a lot of space and be quite complicated. A simpler solution is to implement a different subclass for each type that you support.

Most class clusters provide named constructors, such as **+numberWithFloat:**, that create a new instance of the correct subclass. If you create them with **+alloc**, you typically get a placeholder class returned and then get the real object in response to the initialize message.

The example is a **Pair** class. This does not declare any instance variables and is never used directly. If you send a **+alloc** message to this class, you get a *singleton* instance. When you

send it an initialization message, you get an
instance of one of the two private subclasses.

```
61   @implementation IntPair
62   - (Pair*)initWithInt: (int)a int: (int)b
63   {
64     first = a;
65     second = b;
66     return self;
67   }
68   - (NSString*)description
69   {
70     return [NSString stringWithFormat: @"(%d, %d)",
71         first, second];
72   }
73   - (float)firstFloat { return (float)first; }
74   - (float)secondFloat { return (float)second; }
75   - (int)firstInt { return first; }
76   - (int)secondInt { return second; }
77   @end
```

From: classCluster.m

Each of these concrete subclasses is quite simple.
They both declare two instance variables: **int**s
in one, **float**s in the other. They each provide
a single initializer, which is called only from the
superclass, and they then override the methods.

This example doesn't provide any useful
methods in the superclass. In a real
implementation, you might see methods for
comparison or arithmetic implemented in the
superclass, in terms of the four methods that
are shown here. Alternatively, they might be
provided in a separate category.

The class cluster hides all of the details of the implementation. You can change any aspect of the private subclasses without needing to modify or even recompile code that uses them. This is one of the reasons why code reuse is a lot more common in Objective-C than in languages like C++. It is very easy to produce code in Objective-C that has a public interface and a private implementation, without any code that uses it depending on any aspects of the implementation.

Subclassing a class cluster usually requires implementing a small number of *primitive methods*. The other methods in the superclass are all implemented in terms of this core functionality. We'll look at this in more detail in the Subclassing Collections section in Chapter 7.

If you want to create a new subclass of **NSString**, for example, you must implement **-length** and **-characterAtIndex:**. All other methods in this class just call these two. A more efficient implementation will also implement **-getCharacters:range:**.

Using Run Loops

18
```
[[NSRunLoop currentRunLoop] run];
```

From: timer.m

The design pattern that defines the structure of most nontrivial Objective-C programs is the *run loop*. A run loop, in the general case, waits for data from one or more event sources, and then executes code in response to them, giving an *event driven programming* model.

The Foundation framework provides a run loop implementation in the **NSRunLoop** class. If you are writing an application, you will typically get an instance of this created for you automatically. You may also create one explicitly in command-line tools.

The main run loop in an application listens for events from the window server, corresponding to keypresses, mouse movements, touch events, and so on. Various other classes add event sources to the run loop implicitly. The **NSTimer** class, which we'll look at in Chapter 8, adds a timer event source to the run loop, for example, allowing you to perform some action at a specific time.

The notification mechanism, covered in Chapter 16, lets you deliver notifications of arbitrary events within your program via the run loop, and you can also register for notifications of activity on file descriptors with **NSFileHandle**.

The run loop itself is related to memory management. Each run loop iteration has its own autorelease pool. This means that objects that are sent an **-autorelease** message during a run loop iteration will be destroyed (unless retained elsewhere) at the end of the iteration. Because of this, and the fact that the run loop is used for delivering events from user input, it is a good idea to keep the amount of work done in a single run loop iteration as small as possible.

In most programs, you won't need to interact with the run loop directly. It sits in the background, while other classes provide a more convenient interface.

Numbers

One of the big differences between Objective-C and Smalltalk is that Objective-C inherits the full range of primitive (non-object) C types. These are, in ascending order of size, **char**, **short**, **int**, **long** and **long long** integers, with both **signed** and **unsigned** variants, as well as two floating-point types: **float** and **double**.

These all behave exactly as they do in C, complete with type promotion rules. You'll also find that Objective-C compilers support a **long double** type, which is architecture-dependent.

Note that this is very similar to Java, where you have a small selection of non-object types, but with some very important differences. In Java, the *intrinsic types* are defined to be a fixed size. In C, they are defined to have a minimum precision. For example, the specification says that an **int** has "the natural size suggested by the architecture of the execution environment," whereas in Java it is explicitly defined as a "32-bit signed two's complement integer."

As well as the primitive types, C supports defining new names for the existing types via the **typedef** keyword. The most common reason for this is that the specification does not require a particular size for any of the standard types, merely that each must be at least as big as the previous one. In particular, there are platforms currently deployed where **int** is 16, 32, and 64 bits, so you can't rely on any specific size for these.

OS X supports ILP32 and LP64 modes. This shorthand is used to describe which of the C types have which sizes. ILP32 means that **int**s, **long**s, and pointers are 32 bits. LP64 means that **long**s and pointers are 64-bit quantities, and that, implicitly, other values are smaller. Microsoft Windows, in contrast, is an LLP64 platform on 64-bit architectures; both **int** and **long** remain 32 bits and only pointers and **long long**s are 64 bits. This causes a problem if you assumed that you could safely cast a pointer to **long**—something that works on almost every platform in the world, including Win32, but does not work on Win64.

The problem of casting a pointer to an integer is a serious one. The **long long** type is at least 64 bits, so on any current platform it is guaranteed to be big enough to store any pointer, but on any 32- or 16-bit platform it can be much too big. C99 introduced the `intptr_t` typedef, which is exactly the size of a pointer. Apple introduced an equivalent: `NSInteger`. This is used throughout the Cocoa frameworks and is always the same size as a pointer. There is also an unsigned version, `NSUInteger`.

In GUI code, you will often come across `CGFloat` or `NSFloat`. These are equivalent to each other. Both are the size of a pointer, making them **float**s on 32-bit platforms and **double**s on 64-bit ones.

Storing Numbers in Collections

```
6    NSMutableArray *array = [NSMutableArray array];
7    [array addObject: [NSNumber numberWithInt: 12]];
```

From: numberInArray.m

All of the standard Objective-C collection classes let you store objects, but often you want to store primitive types in them as well. The solution to this is *boxing*—wrapping a primitive type up in an object.

The `NSValue` class hierarchy is used for this. `NSValue` is a class designed to wrap a single primitive value. This class is quite generic, and is an example of a *class cluster*. When you create an instance of an `NSValue`, you will get back some subclass, specialized for storing different kinds of data. If you store a pointer in an NSValue, you don't want the instance to take up as much space as one containing an NSRect— a C structure containing four NSFloats.

One concrete subclass of NSValue is particularly important: NSNumber. This class is intended to wrap single numerical values and can be initialized from any of the C standard integer types.

The designated constructor for both of these classes is +valueWithBytes:objCType. The first argument is a pointer to some value and the second is the *Objective-C type encoding* of the type. Type encodings are strings representing a particular type. They are used a lot for introspection in Objective-C; you can find out the types of any method or instance variable in a class as a type encoding string and then parse this to get the relevant compile-time types.

You can get the type encoding of any type with the @encode() directive. This is analogous to sizeof() in C, but instead of returning the size as an integer it returns the type encoding as a C string. One very convenient trick when working with type encodings is to use the typeof() GCC extension. This returns the type of an expression. You can combine it with @encode(), like this:

```
NSValue *value =
  [NSValue valueWithBytes: &aPrimitive
      objCType: @encode(typeof(aPrimitive))];
```

This snippet will return an NSValue wrapping

aPrimitive, and will work regardless of the type of the primitive. You could wrap this in a macro, but be careful not to pass it an expression with side effects if you do.

Note that you have to pass a pointer to the primitive value. This method will use the type encoding to find out how big the primitive type is and will then copy it.

More often, you will use one of the other constructors. For example, if you want to create an **NSNumber** instance from an integer, you would do so like this:

```
NSNumber *twelve = [NSNumber numberWithInt:
    12];
```

The resulting object can then be added to a collection. Unlike **NSValue**, **NSNumber** instances are ordered, so you can sort collections containing **NSNumber** instances.

The **numberArray.m** example stores a group of **NSNumber** instances in an array and then sorts them using the **-compare:** selector. As you can see from the output, the ordering is enforced irrespective of how the number was created.

```
6   NSArray *a = [NSArray arrayWithObjects:
7     [NSNumber numberWithUnsignedLongLong:
          ULLONG_MAX],
8     [NSNumber numberWithInt: -2],
9     [NSNumber numberWithFloat: 300.057],
10    [NSNumber numberWithInt: 1],
11    [NSNumber numberWithDouble: 200.0123],
12    [NSNumber numberWithLongLong: LLONG_MIN],
13    nil];
14  NSArray *sorted =
15    [a sortedArrayUsingSelector: @selector(compare
        :)];
16  NSLog(@"%@", sorted);
```

From: numberArray.m

```
1   2010-03-15 14:50:48.166 a.out[51465:903] (
2       "-9223372036854775808",
3       "-2",
4       1,
5       "200.0123",
6       "300.057",
7       18446744073709551615
8   )
```

Output from: numberArray

Performing Decimal Arithmetic

```
6   NSDecimalNumber *one =
7     [NSDecimalNumber one];
8   NSDecimalNumber *fortyTwo =
9     [NSDecimalNumber decimalNumberWithString: @"42"
          ];
10  NSDecimalNumber *sum =
11    [one decimalNumberByAdding: fortyTwo];
12  NSDecimal accumulator = [sum decimalValue];
13  NSDecimal temp = [fortyTwo decimalValue];
14  NSDecimalMultiply(&accumulator, &accumulator, &
         temp, NSRoundPlain);
15  temp = [one decimalValue];
16  NSDecimalAdd(&accumulator, &accumulator, &temp,
         NSRoundPlain);
17  NSDecimalNumber *result =
18    [NSDecimalNumber decimalNumberWithDecimal:
          accumulator];
```

From: decimal.m

C gives you two options for working with
numbers: integers and floating-point values.
Floating-point values are made of two
components: a mantissa and an exponent.
Their value is two to the power of the exponent,
multiplied by the mantissa.

The problem with floating-point values is that
they are binary. This means that their precision
is defined in terms of binary digits, which is
not always what you want. For a financial
application, for example, you may need to store
amounts to exactly four decimal places. This is
not possible with floating-point values; a value
such as 0.1 cannot be represented by any finite

binary floating-point, just as 0.1 in base three (one third) cannot be represented by any finite decimal sequence.

A binary number is the sum of a set of powers of two, just as a decimal number is a sum of powers of ten. With fractional values, the digits after the radix point indicate halves, quarters, eighths, and so on. If you try to create a value of 0.1 by adding powers of two, you never succeed, although you get progressively closer. Exactly the same thing happens when you try to create a third by adding powers of ten (a three tenths, plus three hundredths, plus three thousands, and so on).

One solution is to use fixed-point arithmetic. Rather than storing dollars, you might store hundredths of a cent. You must then remember to normalize your values, and you are limited by the range of an integer type. Objective-C provides another option: decimal floating-point types.

The NSDecimal type is a C structure that represents a decimal value. Somewhat strangely, there is no C API for creating these. You must create an **NSDecimalNumber** instance and then send it a **-decimalValue** message.

You then have two choices for arithmetic. **NSDecimalNumber** instances are immutable. You can create new ones as a result of arithmetic—for example, by sending a **decimalNumberByAdding:** message to one.

Alternatively, you can use the C API, which modifies the value of the structure directly.

If you are just performing one arithmetic operation and then storing the result in an object, the first option is simpler. If you are doing a number of steps then it is faster to use the C APIs. Because these modify the structure, they do not require you to create a new object for each intermediate step.

Note: The C1X specification includes decimal number types, and some compilers support these as an extension. The NSDecimal type is not compatible with these. On most platforms this is not important. If you are targeting something like IBM's POWER6, which has hardware for decimal arithmetic, then it is better to use the decimal types directly.

Neither of these is especially fast. The decimal number is represented as an array of digits, and these are operated on in pairs, after the two numbers have been normalized. You can expect to get similar performance to a software floating-point implementation—possibly slightly worse as NSDecimal is not widely used and therefore has not been the focus of much optimization effort.

NSDecimalNumber is a subclass of NSNumber, so all of the ways of converting NSNumbers to strings that we'll look at in the next section work as expected. You can also convert them to

C primitive types using the standard methods for accessing these on number objects, but these methods may truncate or approximate the decimal value.

Converting Between Strings and Numbers

```
6    int answer = [@"42" intValue];
7    NSString *answerString =
8       [NSString stringWithFormat: @"%d", answer];
9    NSNumber *boxedAnswer =
10      [NSNumber numberWithInt: answer];
11   NSCAssert([answerString isEqualToString:
12      [boxedAnswer stringValue]],
13      @"Both strings should be the same");
```

From: strtonum.m

There are several ways of converting between a number and a string. A lot of objects that represent simple data have methods like −intValue, for returning an integer representation of the receiver.

NSString has several methods in this family. If you have a string that contains a numerical value, you can send it a −doubleValue, −floatValue, −intValue, or −longLongValue message to convert it to any of these types. In 64-bit safe versions of Foundation, you can also send it an −integerValue message. This will return an NSInteger.

There are a few ways of going in the

opposite direction, getting a string from an integer. We look at one in Chapter 6: The +stringWithFormat: method on NSString lets you construct a string from any primitive C types, just as you would construct a C string with sprintf().

If you already have a number in an NSNumber instance, there are two ways of getting a string, one of which is a wrapper around the other. The -descriptionWithLocale: method returns a string generated by formatting the number according to the specified locale.

In fact, this doesn't do the translation itself. It sends an -initWithFormat:locale: message to a new NSString. The format string depends on the type of the number: for example, a double will be converted using the @"%0.16g" format string. This uses up to 16 significant figures and an exponent if required.

The decimal separator depends on the locale. If you send an NSNumber a -stringValue message, this is the equivalent to sending a -descriptionWithLocale: message with nil as the argument. This uses the *canonical locale*, which means without any localization, so the result will be the same on any platform.

Reading Numbers from Strings

```objectivec
6    NSScanner *parser =
7      [NSScanner scannerWithString: @"1 plus 2"];
8
9    int operands[2];
10   NSString *operation;
11
12   [parser setCharactersToBeSkipped:
13     [NSCharacterSet whitespaceCharacterSet]];
14
15   [parser scanInt: operands];
16   [parser scanCharactersFromSet:
17     [NSCharacterSet letterCharacterSet]
18             intoString: &operation];
19   [parser scanInt: operands+1];
```

From: scanner.m

Two of the first things any C programmer learns
to use are the **printf()** and **scanf()** functions.
These are very, very similar—one is almost an
inverse of the other—and they let you construct
formatted strings and parse data from them.
We've already seen that **NSString** has a rough
analogue of **sprintf()**, so you can construct
strings from format strings and variables, but
what is the Objective-C equivalent of **sscanf()**?
How, given a string, do we parse values from it?

The answer lies in the **NSScanner** class. This
class is a very powerful tokenizer class. You
create an instance of **NSScanner** attached to
a string and then scan values from it, one at a
time.

The messages you send to a scanner all have the

same form. They take a pointer to a variable and return a **BOOL**, indicating whether they succeeded. The scanner stores the current scanning index in the string, and only increments it on a successful scan, so you can try parsing the next characters in different ways. You can also implement read-ahead and backtracking quite easily with **NSScanner**. If you send it a –scanLocation message, it returns the current index in the string. You can then try scanning a few things, get to an error, and backtrack by sending it a –setScanLocation: message, resetting the old index.

One of the most powerful methods in **NSScanner** is –scanCharactersFromSet:intoString:. This reads a string from the current scanning point until it encounters a character not present in the specified set. As we will see in Chapter 6, you can construct **NSCharacterSet** instances with any arbitrary set of characters, or you can use one of the standard ones.

The example at the start of this section reads a number, then a word, then another number from a string. The number is read using the built in –scanInt: method, but the word is a bit more complex. It uses an NSCharacterSet, in this case the set of all letters.

This isn't the only **NSCharacterSet** used in this example. This scanner is also configured to skip whitespace. The **setCharactersToBeSkipped:** message sent to the scanner tells it to ignore any characters in the set passed as the argument. Passing the whitespace character set tells it to skip any whitespace that occurs between calls. If there are characters in this set at the position where the scanner starts reading when you send it a scan message, it will skip past them. It will not skip these characters while parsing a token, so putting "1 2" in the string would be read as two separate numbers, not as 12.

6

Manipulating Strings

Objective-C provides two sorts of strings: C strings and Objective-C strings, also called *string objects*. As a compiler extension, GCC also lets you use Pascal strings, but these are rare and are only supported for compatibility with Pascal libraries.

A C string is a very primitive data type. It is an array of characters, terminated by a NULL byte. It has no concept of character encodings, and can be used to store any sequence of bytes that does not contain a zero byte. UTF-8 was specifically designed to be usable with C strings: It is a variable-width encoding that does not use zero bytes, even in multibyte sequences.

An Objective-C string is a higher-level abstraction. It is accessed as a sequence of UTF-16 characters, but its internal representation is private. If you compile Objective-C for the GNU runtime, constant strings are represented by an instance of a class with three instance variables: the **isa** pointer, a pointer to a C string, and an integer containing the length of the C string. The runtime library will set the **isa** pointer to the correct class when the module is loaded.

When you access individual characters in an Objective-C string, you use the **unichar** type. This represents a single UTF-16 character. Note that UTF-16 is also a variable-length encoding, and that a single Unicode character may be more than one UTF-16 character. To make matters more confusing, combining marks like accents may mean that more than one Unicode character is used to represent a single glyph.

Creating Constant Strings

```
4   const char* cstring = "C string";
5   NSString *objcstring = @"Objective-C string";
6   CFStringRef cfstring = CFSTR("Core Foundation
        string");
```

From: constantStrings.m

On OS X, Objective-C strings are *toll-free bridged* with *Core Foundation (CF)* strings. Constant CF strings are represented in a similar way to GNU runtime Objective-C strings, but with a few differences. Their **isa** pointer is set to an external reference present in the Core Foundation framework, so they don't require the

Objective-C runtime or Foundation framework to be linked in order to work. They also have a flags field, allowing their internal representation to be either UTF-8 or UTF-16, depending on which is more efficient for their contents.

Constant Objective-C strings are created by prefixing a constant C string literal with an at symbol, as in @*"string"*. You can also create constant Core Foundation strings by using the CFSTR() macro, in both C and Objective-C code. This macro calls a compiler built-in function which generates a constant string object.

Comparing Strings

```
6    NSString *twelve = @"12";
7    NSString *twelveFromInt =
8      [NSString stringWithFormat: @"%d", 12];
9    NSNumber *numberTwelve =
10     [NSNumber numberWithInt: 12];
11
12   if ([twelve isEqualToString: twelveFromInt])
13     NSLog(@"Both strings are equal");
14   if (twelve == twelveFromInt)
15     NSLog(@"Both strings are identical");
16   if (twelve == @"12")
17     NSLog(@"Constant strings are identical");
18   if ([twelve isEqual: numberTwelve])
19     NSLog(@"String is equal to number");
```

From: CompareStrings.m

The simplest and most obvious way of comparing strings for equality is to use the C comparison operator, ==. Unfortunately, this actually does work sometimes, which can lead to some subtle bugs. It will test whether two objects are identical, rather than equal. It will test whether they are the same object, not whether they are objects with equal values.

Comparing two pointers is much faster than comparing two strings, and even faster than sending a message. In some cases, it may be faster to try a pointer comparison first. The result of the pointer comparison is the knowledge that the two strings are the same or that they might be the same. It won't ever tell you that they are definitely different. This can make code faster, if you are comparing identical strings a lot, but is usually an example of *premature optimization*.

If you want to test two strings for equality, you should use the -isEqualToString: method. Note that this expects the argument to be another Objective-C string. You can compare any two Objective-C objects by sending them -isEqual: messages, but it is up to the receiver to decide which other objects it considers to be equal.

In the sample at the start of this section, the compiler will typically combine the constant strings, so that **twelve** and the literal @*"12"* will be the same object. This is not guaranteed, but there is no good reason for the compiler not to do it.

The comparison between the string and the
NSNumber instance is more interesting. You'd
expect this to compare the string to the result
of sending -stringValue to the number, but it
doesn't.

This is important, because equality has to be
commutative. If [a isEqual: b], then a lot of
code will assume that [b isEqual: a]. This is
especially true in collection classes. If you insert
two objects into an NSMutableSet, for example,
where the equality holds in one direction but not
the other, then the result is undefined.

Often, when you want to compare strings—
or, indeed, any objects—you want to find out
not just whether they are equal, but their
ordering. This is where things start to get
a little complicated for strings. Given two
numbers, there is a single canonical ordering
between them. For strings, there are several well-
defined strong orderings. Which order should
"etoile," "Étoilé," and "Etoile" be arranged in?

If you are doing a case-insensitive comparison,
the first and last ones will have equal rank.
Whether accented letters come immediately
before or after their unaccented variants, or
before or after all unaccented letters, depends
on your locale. When you have a list of files, the
user might get irritated if you sort "file10" before
"file2," even though that's the dictionary order
of the two filenames.

For simple comparisons, based solely on the

character values, you can use the −`compare:` method. This, like all other comparison results, returns an `NSComparisonResult`, an enumerated type with three possible values: `NSOrderedAscending`, `NSOrderedSame`, and `NSOrderedDescending`. If you are presenting data to the user, you should use −`localizedCompare:` instead. This will return the ordering of the two strings according to the rules defined for the user's chosen language. Both of these are wrappers around this general comparison method:

```
- (NSComparisonResult)
    compare: (NSString*)aString
    options: (NSStringCompareOptions)mask
      range: (NSRange)range
     locale: (id)locale;
```

This allows you to specify a set of options, such as `NSNumericSearch` for sorting 10 after 9, and `NSCaseInsensitiveSearch` for ignoring case. Passing a range as the third parameter allows you to restrict the comparison to a substring in the receiver, and passing a locale lets you specify the ordering rules for non-ASCII characters. It's worth noting that normally passing `nil` as a locale means either use the current locale or the *canonical locale*. In this case, passing `nil` means use the canonical locale and perform numeric comparisons on the character values.

Processing a String One Character at a Time

```
7   for (NSUInteger i=0 ; i<[aString length] ; i++)
8   {
9      unichar c =
10       [aString characterAtIndex: i];
11         // Process c
12  }
```

From: stringIterateSlow.m

The NSString class is a *class cluster*. It is an abstract class, and when you create one you get an instance of some private subclass. Two primitive methods must be implemented by any NSString subclass: -length and -characterAtIndex:. The first of these returns the length, and the second returns the character at a specific index in the string.

If you need to do something with every character in the string, you can iterate over it in a simple loop, calling this method repeatedly. This is quite inefficient, because it requires a message send for each character. This is significantly more expensive than accessing characters in a C string. This version also sends a -length message for every character, which is only required if the length might change during iteration.

One alternative is to get a C string and work on that. You could, for example, send a -UTF8String message to the string and then process the returned C string. Although this sounds reasonable, remember that the string may be quite large and it may not be stored in UTF-8, so the object may need to convert its internal representation to UTF-8, allocate memory to store it, and then have that memory cleaned up by the autorelease pool (or the garbage collector) later.

The most efficient way of accessing the characters in a string is `-getCharacters:range:`. Methods in Objective-C that start with `get` usually take a pointer to some space allocated by the caller and return the data in that. In this case, the first argument is a pointer to a buffer of `unichar`s, which must be big enough to store the requested number of characters.

The next example uses this mechanism to count the number of semicolons in the source file. First it loads the source code into a string, then it gets the characters ten at a time. Note the double loop structure. The outer loop gets blocks of characters and then the inner loop iterates over the block. This same structure is generated by the compiler when you use *fast enumeration* to iterate over a collection.

This requires one message send for every ten characters. You can trade some more speed for a bit more space by increasing the size of the buffer. Note that this buffer is allocated on the stack. This is fast, but you should be

```
11    int semicolons = 0;
12
13    NSUInteger length = [str length];
14    NSRange range = { 0, 10 };
15    while (range.location < length)
16    {
17      unichar buffer[10];
18      if (range.location + range.length > length)
19      {
20        range.length = length - range.location;
21      }
22      [str getCharacters: buffer range: range];
23      range.location += 10;
24      for (unsigned i=0 ; i<range.length ; i++)
25      {
26        unichar c = buffer[i];
27        if (c == ';')
28        {
29          semicolons++;
30        }
31      }
32    }
33    printf("Source file contained %d semicolons\n",
34        semicolons);
```

From: StringIterate.m

careful to make sure you correctly set the range.
Otherwise, you might potentially introduce some
security holes into your application.

Remember that string objects hide their
encoding. This code will work irrespective of
how the string is stored internally. If it is 7-bit
ASCII or UTF-8, converting most characters to
UTF-16 is very fast. If it's something like Mac
Roman, it may take slightly longer, but it's still

quite quick.

Converting String Encodings

```
5   NSString *str =
6     [NSString stringWithUTF8String:
7     "some text in a C string"];
8   const char *utf16 =
9     [str cStringUsingEncoding:
          NSUTF16StringEncoding];
10  const char *utf32 =
11    [str cStringUsingEncoding:
          NSUTF32StringEncoding];
12  const char *macRoman =
13    [str cStringUsingEncoding:
          NSMacOSRomanStringEncoding];
```

From: encodings.m

In OpenStep, two of the most common methods on **NSString** were **-cString** and **+stringWithCString:**. These converted between a C string and an Objective-C string. The problem with these methods was that C strings are not encoding aware.

A C string is an array of bytes. You can store any kind of character data in them that you like. All of the operations on them are defined externally, so the knowledge of the character encoding is extrinsic to the string. This is the opposite of how an Objective-C string works.

When you converted a C string to or from an Objective-C string, it had to know what the

encoding of the C string was. The C standard
library functions check an environment variable
to find out what this should be. Unfortunately,
this causes all sorts of problems. If you read
some data from a socket or a file and then
construct an Objective-C string from it with
these functions, you get whatever text encoding
your user picked, not the encoding selected by
the person who created the file.

These methods are all now deprecated, and in
their place are methods that take an explicit
encoding parameter. One thing to remember is
that the default for any multibyte encoding is
big-endian, which made sense on the Motorola
68000 series and RISC workstations where
Objective-C gained popularity, but is less
sensible on little-endian x86 processors.

The most common text encoding in countries
that use some variant of the Latin alphabet
is UTF-8. This lets you represent any of the
ASCII characters in a single byte and most
other common characters in two.[1] **NSString**
has convenience methods for getting and
setting UTF-8 encoded data: **-UTF8String** and
+stringWithUTF8String:. In most code, you
can use these whenever you are converting to or
from C strings.

To create a string object from a C string
in some other encoding, you use the

---

[1]If you are using ideographic characters, UTF-8 is
quite inefficient.

`+stringWithCString:encoding:` method.
The first argument to this is the C string,
and the second is a member of an enumerated
type representing the encoding. If the data
is coming from an older Mac, you may
want to use `NSMacOSRomanStringEncoding`,
which was the default encoding before Mac
OS got Unicode support. If you need to
interoperate with old Windows systems,
`NSWindowsCP1252StringEncoding` is the
encoding that you will need in most of the
world. Newer Windows systems will use UTF-
16, but they prefer the little-endian version,
`NSUTF16LittleEndianStringEncoding`.

If you are storing string data in a particular
encoding, you will often use instances of `NSData`,
rather than pointers. This is a very simple
class, which encapsulates a region of memory:
a pointer and a size. Because it is an object,
you can introspect it, use reference counting to
handle destruction, and store it in collections.
This makes it more convenient, in a number of
cases, than using pointers directly.

Trimming Strings

```
6   NSString *str =
7     @"  a String with leading spaces   ";
8   str = [str
9     stringByTrimmingCharactersInSet:
10      [NSCharacterSet whitespaceCharacterSet]];
11  str = [str substringFromIndex: 2];
12  NSCAssert([str isEqualToString:
13     @"String with leading spaces"],
14    @"Trimming failed");
```

From: trim.m

Often, when you have a string, you want to trim
the ends, removing either a fixed number of
characters or characters from a particular set. A
common example of the second case is removing
leading and trailing whitespace from a string.

Objective-C string objects support quite a few
methods for doing this. If you just want to
remove the trailing or leading characters from
a string, the **-substringWithRange:** method
on **NSString** is the most useful. This will
create a new string object containing a range of
characters in another string. This is a very cheap
operation on immutable strings; it just returns
a string object that references the data in the
original string, it doesn't copy the string. When
you call it on a mutable string, however, it must
copy the characters.

To remove characters from a particular set, you
need to understand **NSCharacterSet** objects. As
its name implies, this class encapsulates a set of

characters. You can create these from a string, but there are also a number of predefined ones that represent a particular well-defined set of characters.

This class is used in a similar way to the ctype.h functions in C. You can send it a −characterIsMember: message to test whether a single character is a member of the set. Calling the ispunct() C library function, for example, is equivalent to sending a −characterIsMember: message to the object obtained by sending a +punctuationCharacterSet message to NSCharacterSet.

The Objective-C version is more verbose, but is more generic. Character set objects can be passed around your code easily. The NSString class uses them in a number of places. You can ask for the range within a string of characters in a given set, or split a string using a character set to define the separators, for example.

Splitting Strings

```
6    NSString *str =
7      @"A String with\twords and spaces";
8    NSArray *wordsWithTab = [str
9      componentsSeparatedByString: @" "];
10   NSArray *words = [str
11     componentsSeparatedByCharactersInSet:
12       [NSCharacterSet whitespaceCharacterSet]];
```

From: split.m

There are three ways of splitting strings in Objective-C. The first is obvious: Simply iterate over the characters until you find a convenient place for a split and then use -substringWithRange: to create the new token. This will work in the general case, but is quite a lot of effort for something that should be trivial.

In C, you can use the strsep() function, or the deprecated strtok() function, to split a string anywhere that a character in a specific set is found. The -componentsSeparatedByCharactersInSet: method on NSString works in almost exactly the same way, although it takes an NSCharacterSet as an argument instead of a string.

You can make this method behave like strtok_r() by constructing a character set using +characterSetWithCharactersInString:. The NSString method returns an NSArray with the substrings. This works exactly like the C functions; you get empty strings wherever there are two adjacent separator characters.

Alternatively, you can split a string based on occurrences of a specific substring. This is very useful when you have separators composed of several characters.

Copying Strings

```objc
NSString *staticString = @"a string";
NSString *constantString =
  [staticString copy];
NSString *stringAlias =
  [constantString retain];
NSMutableString *mutableString =
    [stringAlias mutableCopy];
NSMutableString *mutableStringAlias =
    [mutableString retain];
```

From: stringcopy.m

One of the places were C++ tends to be much slower than it should is in the handling of strings. In any environment where you have pure manual memory management, there is a tendency to defensively copy objects to maintain clear ownership rules.

In Objective-C, this is less common, and more code suffers from the opposite problem: retaining references to mutable objects when it should have copies. When you send a -copy message to an NSString, it has the same effect as sending -retain.

Why, you might be wondering, do we have two methods that do the same thing? The answer is simple: NSMutableString is a subclass of NSString. If you send a -retain message to an NSMutableString, you increment the reference count. If you send a -copy message, you get a new object. It can be even more complex than that because some NSMutableString concrete subclasses support copy-on-write behavior, so you will get two objects referencing the same data, and only get a real copy made when you modify one of them.

Because NSMutableString is a subclass of NSString, you can pass a pointer to an NSMutableString anywhere that expects an NSString pointer. If you expect an immutable string and are given one, it doesn't matter whether you copy the object or just make another reference to it. If, on the other hand, you are given a mutable string, you don't want to just keep a reference to it or you might end up with it being modified later.

It's important to remember that sending a -copy message to any NSString subclass will always return an immutable string. If you want a mutable string, you must use -mutableCopy instead.

Note: If you are coming from Java, remember that NSString is roughly equivalent to the Java String class and NSMutableString is roughly equivalent to the Java StringBuffer class. Objective-C has no equivalent of the **final** keyword, so NSString may—and does—have subclasses, and you can use mutable strings anywhere you would otherwise use an immutable string.

This pattern is found in several places in the

Foundation framework. Most classes that have an immutable superclass and a mutable subclass will implement the **NSMutableCopying** protocol. Sending mutable or immutable instances of them a **-mutableCopying** message will give you an instance of the mutable subclass.

Creating Strings from Templates

```
6    int a = 12;
7    float b = 42.0;
8    const char *cString = "words";
9    id object = [NSObject new];
10   NSString *string =
11     [NSString stringWithFormat:
12       @"%d, %f, %s, %@",
13       a, b, cString, object];
```

From: formatstring1.m

If you come from a C background, one of the first functions you learned about was probably **printf()**. This is a *variadic function* that takes a *format string* as the first argument. The contents of the format string then define the types of the other arguments.

Objective-C, as a descendant of C, inherits the idea of a format string. Objective-C format strings are almost exactly like C format strings, but with one addition. The %@ format specifier indicates that the matching argument is an object.

Objects are expected to know how to describe

themselves. Every object should respond to a **-description** message, which returns an **NSString** describing the object. A lot of classes inherit this from **NSObject**, which just returns the class name and the object's address in memory. Others provide something more convenient. For example, the collection classes dump their contents as NeXT-style *property lists*.

Note: The *GNU debugger (gdb)* has some built-in support for –description methods. When you use the print-object command (which can be abbreviated to po) on an object, it will call its –description method. Be careful when doing this, because it will run some code in the debugged process, which may also contain bugs. However, when it works, it can be very helpful. We'll look at debugging more in Chapter 18.

You can create Objective-C string objects from format strings using a *variadic method* that behaves like **asprintf()**. The first argument is an Objective-C string containing some format specifiers, and the remaining arguments are the variables that will be used in place of the format specifiers. The formatstring.m example shows how you can use format strings with **NSString**.

This example constructs a string from the arguments provided to the executable and then writes it to the standard error. Note that we need to create an **NSAutoreleasePool** at the

```
3    int main(int argc, char **argv)
4    {
5      [NSAutoreleasePool new];
6      NSMutableString *str =
7        [NSMutableString stringWithFormat:
8          @"%d arguments: ", argc];
9      for (int i=0 ; i<argc ; i++)
10     {
11       [str appendFormat: @"%s ", argv[i]];
12     }
13     NSLog(@"%@", str);
14     return 0;
15   }
```

From: formatstring.m

start of this program. Using format strings
creates some temporary objects, which are
autoreleased. If you don't have an autorelease
pool, you will get a warning that these objects
are leaked. In this trivial program, they are
leaked anyway; there's no point in telling the
autorelease pool to collect them because the
operating system will reclaim the memory when
the process exits anyway.

This example first creates a mutable string
containing the number of arguments passed to
the program. It then loops over the remaining
arguments, appending each (as a C string) to the
mutable string. Finally, it passes the result to
NSLog().

The NSLog() function also uses format strings.
It's tempting to just pass **str** as the first

argument. This will work fine until someone
uses a string with a percent symbol in it as an
argument to this program. Then the function
will look at the second argument and try to
interpret it. Unfortunately, there is no second
argument, so will read a random value from
a register. If it's interpreting this as some
kind of number, it's not a big problem. If it's
interpreting it as a pointer (to a C string or
Objective-C object), it will almost certainly
crash. By passing @"%@" we tell NSLog() that
there is only one real argument, and that it's an
object.

Matching Patterns in Strings

```
 8   NSRegularExpression *regex = [NSRegularExpression
 9     regularExpressionWithPattern: @"abcd*"
10                          options: 0
11                            error: NULL];
12   NSMutableString *str = [@"abcddd fish, wibble
         abcd, abc, foo" mutableCopy];
13   NSRange all = NSMakeRange(0, [str length]);
14   [regex enumerateMatchesInString: str
15                           options: 0
16                             range: all
17                        usingBlock:
18     ^(NSTextCheckingResult *result, NSMatchingFlags
           flags, BOOL *stop)
19     {
20       NSLog(@"Matched range: %@", NSStringFromRange
             ([result range]));
21     }];
22
23   NSLog(@"Copy with replacement: %@",
24     [regex stringByReplacingMatchesInString: str
25                                     options: 0
26                                       range: all
27                                withTemplate: @"foo"
                                            ]);
```

From: regex.m

If you've used a language like Perl or JavaScript,
then you're probably accustomed to using
regular expressions for pattern matching in
strings. Recent versions of the Foundation
framework include the **NSRegularExpression**
class, which is a thin wrapper around the
International Components for Unicode (ICU)
regular expression code.

This class has a single primitive method, which takes a block as the final argument and calls it once for every match. All the other methods in the class are implemented in terms of this method.

The example at the start of this section shows two common ways of using this class. Both begin by constructing an instance of it, encapsulating a simple regular expression. For efficiency, you should try to reuse regular expression objects, rather than creating them from strings every time. When the instance is created, the input string will be parsed and transformed into a state machine that can quickly run on strings. The regular expression object is immutable and thread safe, so you can store commonly-used patterns in global variables and reuse them repeatedly from multiple threads.

The first way of using the regular expression shows the low-level API. This is passed a block, which is called once for every match. This simple example prints the location of each match within the string.

The higher-level API does the replacement for you. This comes in two flavors, one that takes an NSString and returns a new copy with the result of the replacement and one that takes an NSMutableString and does the replacement in place.

Note that the template used for replacement is not a simple string. It can contain references to

parts of the original regular expression, using the
$n syntax that you'd use in regular expressions
elsewhere.

Storing Rich Text

```
6    NSDictionary *keyword = [[NSDictionary
7       dictionaryWithObject: @"keyword"
8              forKey: @"type"] retain];
9    NSMutableAttributedString *program =
10     [NSMutableAttributedString new];
11
12   NSAttributedString *fragment =
13     [[NSAttributedString alloc]
14       initWithString: @"int"
15         attributes: keyword];
16   [program appendAttributedString: fragment];
```

From: richText.m

A string is just a list of characters. Before
you display a string, you generally need some
other attributes. These attributes describe the
typeface, the size, the alignment and underline
styles, and so on.

If you are writing something that deals with
structured text—for example, HTML or another
form of semantic markup such as DocBook—
then these attributes might be a level 1 heading,
or ordered list.

Foundation provides a class for assigning
arbitrary attributes to strings. The
NSAttributedString class lets you attach

dictionaries to ranges in attributed strings. These dictionaries can contain any arbitrary information that you want, including semantic markup.

AppKit uses this class and defines a few keys for the dictionaries for providing presentation markup. You can use this to attach an `NSFont` instance to a range of text and have the text system in AppKit display that range of the text in the specified font.

The example constructs a fragment of a program as an attributed string, defining attributes for defining keywords. You might then have a transform that takes this attributed string and generates one using presentation attributes for display in a text view, or another one for generating HTML from this markup.

It's important to remember that `NSAttributedString` is generic. You can use it for attaching any attributes that you want to define to ranges in a string.

7

Working with Collections

As with other things we've looked at, there are two kinds of collections in Objective-C: the object-oriented versions and the primitive C types. The former, as usual, is built on top of the latter.

In C, there are two kinds of compound data types: arrays and structures. Arrays are just blocks of memory containing the same sort of data. Structures have a fixed layout and may contain different types as elements.

C composite types are a very thin layer of syntactic sugar on pointer arithmetic. When you access an element in an array, the compiler multiplies the array index by the size of one element and adds this to the pointer to the start of the array. When you access an element in a structure, the compiler adds a fixed offset to the pointer to the start of the structure.

Objective-C collections are higher-level constructs. Each Objective-C collection, like most of the other additions made by Objective-C, is an object. You communicate with them by sending them messages.

The Foundation framework includes a number of collection classes for storing ordered and unordered data, as well as maps or sets of indexes. Most of the collection classes in Objective-C store objects. Unlike C++ STL collections, which need refining for the types they may contain, Objective-C collections are heterogeneous. They may store any kind of Objective-C object.

Most Objective-C collections, like strings, use the *mutable subclass pattern*, where the superclass implements behavior for an immutable collection and a subclass provides a mutable version.

All of the classes that follow this pattern implement the `NSMutableCopying` protocol, meaning that you can send a `-mutableCopy` message to a collection and get a copy that is mutable, even if the original isn't.

Most collections are also *class clusters*. When you create one, you will get some private subclass. The public classes are typically abstract. The user-friendly methods are all implemented in terms of a small number of primitive methods. If you create your own subclass, you will need to implement these methods yourself.

Using Arrays

```
6   NSArray *array = [NSArray arrayWithObjects:
7     @"array", @"containing", @"string", @"objects",
          nil];
8   NSMutableArray *mutable = [array mutableCopy];
9   [mutable sortUsingSelector: @selector(
          localizedCompare:)];
10  [mutable addObject: [NSNumber numberWithInteger:
          12]];
11  [mutable removeAllObjects];
```

From: nsarray.m

In addition to C arrays, Foundation provides
the NSArray class and its mutable subclass
NSMutableArray. These implement an abstract
data type that maps from integers, in a
contiguous range starting at zero, to objects.
Internally, it may be implemented by C
arrays, skip lists, or some other data structure,
depending on how it was created.

For example, if you create an array by appending
two immutable arrays, you may get a composite
array that doesn't store anything internally, and
just accesses the other two arrays. Or you might
get a completely new array, depending on what
the people implementing the relevant NSArray
subclass thought would be more efficient for that
specific case.

The easiest way of creating an Objective-
C array is to use the +arrayWithObjects:
method, implemented by both NSArray and
NSMutableArray. This is another example of

a *variadic method*, taking a list of objects as arguments and using **nil** to signify the end of the list. You must be careful, when using variables as arguments to this method, that none of the variables are **nil**, or the array will see that as the end of the argument list and ignore the later values.

Note: Most Objective-C collections don't allow you to store **nil** as a value. If you need to signify a null value, rather than an absence of a value, you can use the NSNull class. This provides a singleton object that can be accessed with [NSNull null].

Arrays are *class clusters*. The two primitive methods in **NSArray** are **-objectAtIndex** and **-count**. All of the other methods are implemented in terms of these. Some concrete subclasses, of course, will implement more efficient versions, but if you want to create a new **NSArray** subclass, you must implement these two methods if you want the other methods in the superclass to work.

Subclassing **NSMutableArray** is a bit harder; it adds another six primitive methods. Most of the time, however, you will be using arrays, not subclassing them. You can insert an object into a mutable array with either -**addObject:**, which adds it at the end, or -**insertObject:atIndex:**, which inserts it at

the specified index. The latter method moves
all subsequent objects along by one in the
array to make room. To replace an object, use
-replaceObjectAtIndex:withObject:.

Manipulating Indexes

```
13  NSMutableIndexSet *indexSet =
14    [NSMutableIndexSet indexSetWithIndex: 1];
15  [indexSet addIndexesInRange:
16    NSMakeRange(5, 20)];
17  [array removeObjectsAtIndexes:
18    indexSet];
```

From: indexset.m

Arrays are indexed by integers. Often, you want
to do some operation on a group of values in
an array. A special class, called **NSIndexSet**, is
used for storing groups of indexes. Internally,
this stores a set of ranges, so can be quite dense.

A very common use for index sets is to collect a
group of indexes while enumerating an array and
then remove them at the end. Removing objects
from a collection while enumerating it is a bad
idea, and will throw an exception in most cases.
If you add each index that you want to remove
to an index set, you can remove them all at once
when you finish the enumeration.

Operations involving index sets are usually
more efficient than the corresponding operations
involving individual indexes. This is true even

in a relatively naïve implementation, because you need fewer message sends. You also get to avoid some range checking. Each operation on an Objective-C array is bounds checked to make sure that it doesn't refer to an index beyond the end of the array. With an index set, the receiver just has to compare the result of **-lastIndex** with the last index in the array, and then it can operate on every single element in the index set without range checking.

Like other collections, index sets come in mutable and immutable flavors. Most of the time you will use the mutable version. You manipulate it by adding and removing either individual indexes (**NSUInteger**s) or ranges. You can use index sets for storing indexes to anything, but they are most useful in conjunction with **NSArray**s, which have several methods designed to take index sets as arguments. You can often use them as an alternative to creating a subarray if you just want to work on some arbitrary subset of the elements in an array.

Storing Unordered Groups of Objects

```
6    NSArray *array = [NSArray arrayWithObjects:
7      @"set", @"object", @"containing",
8      @"seven", @"objects", @"not",
9      @"eight", @"objects", nil];
10   NSSet *set = [NSSet setWithArray: array];
11   NSMutableSet *mSet = [set mutableCopy];
12   NSCountedSet *cSet =
13     [NSCountedSet setWithArray: array];
```

From: nsset.m

If you want to store a collection of objects
without a defined order, you can use NSSet
and its mutable subclass. This models a
mathematical set, so inserting the same object
twice will only store one copy of it.

How NSSet determines equality between objects
is quite complex. Equality is not the same as
identity; it will not store two copies of the same
object, but it will also not store two objects
with the same value. It determines whether
two objects are equal by sending one of them
an -isEqual: message with the other as an
argument.

The simplest way of implementing NSSet would
be to compare every new object to every existing
object. This would be painfully slow, however,
so fortunately NSSet doesn't work this way.
Instead, it uses the -hash method. Every object
is expected to implement this method and return
an integer hash value.

If two objects are equal, they must have the same hash. Collections such as NSSet put objects into buckets based on their hash values. When testing whether an object is already in the set, it just has to test the objects that have the same hash.

A good hash is, therefore, important for good performance of these collection classes. Fortunately, NSString, which is the most commonly used object in this kind of collection, already has a good hash implementation.

One slight problem with this approach is that an object must not change its hash while it is in a collection. This is impossible to enforce for mutable objects without breaking some of the other rules. It is, therefore, important not to modify objects while they are stored in a set.

One other kind of set is NSCountedSet, which is a subclass of NSMutableSet that supports adding the same object multiple times. This adds one method to NSMutableSet, -countForObject:, which returns the number of times a particular object has been added to the collection.

Note: In Java, and some other languages, a counted set is called a *bag*.

It's worth noting that, because NSCountedSet is a subclass of NSSet, some of its methods are designed to allow NSCountedSet instances to be used in place of NSSet instances. If you send a

−**count** message to any of the sets created in the
example at the start of this section, you will get
the same value. If you iterate over any of the
sets, you will get seven objects. You can only tell
if an object is in the counted set more than once
by sending a -**countForObject:** message to the
set.

Creating a Dictionary

```
6   NSMutableDictionary *dict = [NSMutableDictionary
7     dictionaryWithObjectsAndKeys: @"One", @"1",
8     @"Two", @"2", nil];
9   [dict setObject: @"three" forKey: @"3"];
```

From: dictionary.m

A dictionary, often called a *map* or *associative
array*, provides a collection of objects indexed by
other objects. Most commonly, dictionaries are
indexed by strings. This is not the only option,
but there are some restrictions on the classes
that can be used as keys in dictionaries.

Dictionaries are similar to sets, and the same
constraints apply. Objects used as keys must
implement the −**hash** and −**isEqual:** methods,
returning **YES** on comparison and the same hash
value if they are equal. The hash value must not
change as long as they are in the collection.

Additionally, keys must implement the
NSCopying protocol. When you add a key-value
pair to a dictionary, the value will be retained,

but the key will be copied. This is done to prevent it from being modified accidentally. If you pass an immutable object, such as an `NSString`, this has the same effect as retaining it. If you pass an `NSMutableString`, then the dictionary will use an immutable copy.

Finally, it's worth remembering that only dictionaries that use strings as keys will work with *key-value coding* (see Chapter 11). You should also be very careful when using different classes as keys in the same dictionary that their comparison methods return the correct values when passed instances of the other classes.

The most common method you will use on a dictionary is `-objectForKey:`, which returns the object associated with the given key, or `nil` if there is no object set for that key. For mutable dictionaries, you will typically use the `-setObject:forKey:` method to set key-value pairs in a dictionary.

Iterating Over a Collection

```objc
19   NSLog(@"The Objective-C 1 way:");
20   NSEnumerator *e=[a objectEnumerator];
21   for (id obj=[e nextObject] ;
22        nil!=obj ;
23        obj=[e nextObject])
24   {
25     [obj print];
26   }
27   NSLog(@"Fast enumeration:");
28   for (id obj in a)
29   {
30     [obj print];
31   }
32   NSLog(@"Using blocks:");
33   [a enumerateObjectsUsingBlock:
34     ^(id obj, NSUInteger idx, BOOL *stop)
35     {
36       [obj print];
37     }];
38   NSLog(@"Avoiding enumeration:");
39   [a makeObjectsPerformSelector: @selector(print)];
```

From: enum.m

One of the most common tasks you perform with
collections is to iterate over every element in the
collection and do some processing. There are a
lot of ways of doing this in Objective-C. Because
it's such a common task, new ways of doing it
keep being added.

For arrays, you can go through every single
index from 0 to [array count] and send
an -objectAtIndex: message. This is very
inefficient. The traditional way of enumerating

over a collection is to use an enumeration; an instance of an NSEnumerator subclass.

Note: If you are coming from Java, mentally substitute the word *iterator* for enumerator and you will find most of the patterns you are familiar with still work.

You can get an enumerator for a collection by sending it an –objectEnumerator message. This object is very simple. It responds to only two messages, and you're only ever likely to use one of them: –nextObject. This returns the next object in the collection, or nil if you've already enumerated all of the objects that a collection contains.

With Objective-C 2, Apple introduced *fast enumeration*. You can use this with any collections that implement the NSFastEnumeration protocol. This protocol defines a method for getting several objects with a single message send. The exact number is defined by the caller and the receiver. The compiler allocates a buffer and passes a pointer to it to the receiver. The receiver may then copy some objects into this buffer or, if it stores data internally as a C array (or a group of arrays), return a pointer to its internal store.

The method in this protocol is used by a new flow-control construct, the **for..in** loop. When you use this, the compiler will produce two nested loops. In the outer loop, it will call the fast enumeration method, getting the next few objects from the collection. In the inner loop, it will iterate over this C array.

Note: If you are using automatic reference counting, then the contract for the fast enumeration protocol is stricter. The collection is required to ensure that objects are valid for the duration of the enumeration (or signal that the collection has mutated). Because of this, you are not allowed to assign to the enumeration variable without an explicit qualifier, because if you do, ARC doesn't know how to treat your assignment. In general, it's better to declare a new variable inside the loop for new temporary values.

You can use fast enumeration without compiler support. The GSFastEnumeration.h header in GNUstep provides FOR_IN and END_FOR_IN macros that expand to produce the same code the compiler will use for **for..in** loops. These macros are quite complicated, so it's better to not try calling the fast enumeration methods yourself.

With OS X 10.6, Apple introduced another new way of iterating over collections: using *blocks*. Blocks are a new language extension to C, but designed for close interoperation with Objective-C. Like Objective-C objects, blocks have an **isa** pointer. This points to a private class that implements the NSObject protocol, so you can store blocks in collections. They also support introspection using Objective-C type encodings, although this support is not yet part of their public interface on OS X.

Most of the collection classes now implement methods for enumeration using blocks. Using these can be convenient, although it does limit the portability of your code. You can perform concurrent enumerations with blocks, by passing NSEnumerationConcurrent as the first argument to a method such as -enumerateObjectsWithOptions:usingBlock:. This is generally only likely to give a performance gain if the block will take a long time to execute on each element.

Each collection has different methods for enumeration via blocks. The version for arrays takes the index of the object as an argument, the version for dictionaries takes both the key and value, and so on. These methods will be slower than the other alternatives, because they require the block to be called for each object (which has the same overhead as calling a function), but they can be more convenient.

In some cases, you can avoid enumeration entirely. NSArray, for example, implements a -makeObjectsPerformSelector method, and another version that takes an object as a second argument. If all that you are doing while enumerating is sending a message to each object, you can use these methods instead of creating a loop.

Finding an Object in a Collection

```
6   NSArray *array = [NSArray arrayWithObjects:
7     @"a", @"group", @"of",
8     @"string", @"objects", nil];
9   NSSet *set = [NSSet setWithArray: array];
10  NSUInteger i =
11    [array indexOfObjectIdenticalTo: @"group"];
12  if (NSNotFound == i)
13    i - [array indexOfObject: @"group"|;
14  NSString *original = [set member: @"string"];
```

From: getObject.m

Both **NSArray** and **NSSet** implement the -containsObject: method, which returns **YES** if the collection contains an object that is equal to the argument. This uses the same notion of equality we've already covered in relation to collection classes: Two objects are equal if sending one an -isEqual: message with the other as the argument returns **YES**.

In an array, you probably want to know exactly where the object is, rather than simply whether it is present. There are two methods for telling you this: -indexOfObject: and -indexOfObjectIdenticalTo:. The second of these uses pointer comparison to determine equality.

All of these are slow in arrays. They all require a linear search, and most of them require sending a message to each object. In general, you should only use them in small arrays or infrequently called code paths. If you need to perform this reverse mapping often, you're better off using a dictionary or something similar to store the inverse relationship.

With sets, the performance is somewhat different. Because sets store objects in buckets according to their hash, a set can quickly discount a lot of objects as being different. Obviously, because sets are unordered, there is no set method for looking up the index of an object. There is, however, a method for looking up the stored object that is equal to an object.

The `-member:` method on `NSSet` returns the stored object that is equal to the argument. This is very useful for ensuring uniqueness in objects. The unique.m example shows a method that constructs unique constant string objects from C strings. If you pass the same C string to this method twice, you will get the same `NSString` instance returned both times.

Note that this function is not thread-safe. There is a potential race between testing whether the string is in the set and adding the new one if it isn't. A thread-safe version of this would require you to acquire a lock after the `-member:` call, send this message again, and then finally release the lock after adding the new object.

```
3   static NSMutableSet *unique_strings;
4
5   NSString *uniqueString(const char *str)
6   {
7     NSString *new = [[NSString alloc]
8       initWithUTF8String: str];
9
10    NSString *old =
11      [unique_strings member: new];
12
13    if (nil != old)
14    {
15      [new release];
16      return old;
17    }
18    [unique_strings addObject: new];
19    return new;
20  }
```

From: unique.m

If you are creating a new immutable class, you
may wish to implement something like this in
your constructor. This will trade some speed for
memory usage in construction, but will mean
that you can always use pointer comparisons to
determine equality, which can be a big speed win
overall in some cases.

Subclassing Collections

```
25   - (NSUInteger)count
26   {
27     return [realArray count];
28   }
29   - (id)objectAtIndex: (NSUInteger)anIndex
30   {
31     return
32       [realArray objectAtIndex: anIndex];
33   }
```

From: checkedArray.m

All of the standard collections are *class clusters*. This means that creating a new subclass of them is nontrivial. The superclass is abstract, and the concrete subclasses are private (so you can't subclass them).

Each of the collections documents the methods you must implement in a subclass. The simplest way of doing this is via delegation: just have an object that is the same type as the collection you are subclassing as an instance variable. The typedArray.m example uses this approach.

The TypedArray class is a subclass of NSMutableArray. The **realArray** instance variable in this class is an NSMutableArray. This is created in the class's designated initializer and, just like any other code that creates an NSMutableArray, will really get an instance of one of the concrete subclasses of this class. The other instance variable is a **Class**, which is used to type check objects that are inserted into the array.

```
10   - (id)initWithType: (Class)aClass
11   {
12     if (nil == (self = [super init]))
13     {
14       return nil;
15     }
16     type = aClass;
17     realArray = [NSMutableArray new];
18     return self;
19   }
20   - (void)dealloc
21   {
22     [realArray release];
23     [super dealloc];
24   }
```

From: checkedArray.m

Unlike the standard array classes, which are heterogeneous, this version requires every object you insert to be an instance (or subclass of) the class passed to the initializer. This version will silently fail if you try to insert other objects, but you could easily modify it to throw an exception.

A number of the methods in this class are trivial. The -removeObjectAtIndex: method, for example, just passes the same message to the wrapped array. Others, such as -insertObject:atIndex:, do the type checking and then call the real array.

This example implements all seven of the primitive methods in NSMutableArray. This

```
34   - (void)insertObject: (id)anObject
35               atIndex: (NSUInteger)anIndex
36   {
37     if (![anObject isKindOfClass: type])
38     {
39       return;
40     }
41     [realArray insertObject: anObject
42                     atIndex: anIndex];
43   }
44   - (void)removeObjectAtIndex: (NSUInteger)idx
45   {
46     [realArray removeObjectAtIndex: idx];
47   }
```

From: checkedArray.m

means that all of the other methods declared on
NSArray or NSMutableArray will work correctly.

Note: In C++, the primitive methods would be
pure **virtual** methods in the superclass, and the
compiler would prevent you from instantiating
the superclass directly, or any subclass that
did not implement these methods. There is no
corresponding facility in Objective-C.

A more common reason for subclassing is that
you want to implement a different data structure
for the underlying representation. For example,
if you are going to insert objects at one end of an
array and then remove them from the other, you
might want to use a resizable ring buffer as your

array implementation.

If this is the case, you should still override the same methods, but this time replace them with an implementation in terms of your own storage mechanism. You can then still use your subclass anywhere that the superclass can be used—including passing it to other libraries—but your own storage will be used.

Storing Objective-C Objects in C++ Collections

```
30    std::tr1::unordered_map<id, __weak id,
          object_hash<id>, object_equal<id> > map;
31    @autoreleasepool {
32      NSString *str = [[NSString alloc]
          initWithUTF8String: argv[0]];
33      map[@"arg0"] = str;
34      NSLog(@"%@", map[@"arg0"]);
35      str = nil;
36    }
37    NSLog(@"%@", map[@"arg0"]);
```

From: collection.mm

One of the historical problems with Objective-C++ is the difficulty in interoperability between collection types. Objective-C collections are intended to store Objective-C objects, and therefore, are not usable when storing C++ structures. C++ collections are a bit more flexible. They are implemented as templates; therefore, in theory they can store any type.

In practice, storing Objective-C objects in C++ collections was complicated by memory management. Objective-C objects expect anything that wants to keep an owning reference to them to send a `-retain` message. C++ collections, not being written with Objective-C in mind, did not do this, so you had to be very careful using them with Objective-C++.

With automatic reference counting, this becomes a lot simpler. When you use a C++ template with an Objective-C object type, it is expanded, and every assignment in the template automatically has the relevant reference counting calls inserted around it. This even extends to weak references on systems that support them. The example at the start of this section shows how to use a C++ map type to implement something equivalent to an `NSMapTable` with strong-to-weak pointers.

The C++ `unordered_map` requires two support classes, one for defining equality and one for hashing an object. These are implemented simply wrapping the relevant Objective-C messages.

It's possible to do something similar, although without support for weak pointers, using a C++ smart pointer class, which sends a `-retain` message when constructed and a `-release` message when destroyed. This is likely to be a lot slower, however, because it won't benefit from the ARC optimizations. A typical

```
 8   template <typename X>
 9   struct object_equal
10   {
11     bool operator()(const X s1, const X s2) const
12     {
13       return (s1==s2) || [(id)s1 isEqual:(id)s2];
14     }
15   };
16
17   template <typename X>
18   struct object_hash
19   {
20     size_t operator()(const X s1) const
21     {
22       return (size_t)[(id)s1 hash];
23     }
24   };
```

From: collection.mm

operation on a C++ collection may assign the pointer several times. This will result in a lot of retain and release operations, which the ARC optimizer will then remove where they are redundant. With a smart pointer class, they will generate a lot of message sends.

In C++ terminology, this means that **__unsafe_unretained id** is a *plain old data (POD)* type, while **__weak id** and **__strong id** are non-POD types. They (implicitly) implement overloaded assignment operators and nontrivial copy constructors. If you don't understand what that means, then don't worry; just assume that you can use ARC in C++ and everything works by magic.

Dates and Times

In Objective-C, two concepts fall under the general umbrella of time. One is absolute times, the other is time intervals. Time intervals are easy to work with. They are simple scalar quantities, typically measured in seconds. The NSTimeInterval type is used to store time intervals. This is usually defined as a double-precision floating-point value, which gives enough precision for most uses.

You will find some other ways of representing time intervals in various frameworks. One example is the QTKit on OS X, which stores time intervals as rational numbers. This allows you to repeatedly add them without encountering drift due to floating-point rounding errors, which is very important when dealing with media. Over the length of a film, compound floating-point errors can make the video and audio tracks drift noticeably out of sync.

Time intervals give the difference between two

absolute times. The definition of an absolute
time is quite difficult. Things such as time zones
and even different calendars make it relatively
difficult to define an absolute time. Much of
the code related to times and dates in the
Foundation framework is designed to solve this
problem.

Finding the Current Date

```
6    NSDate *now = [NSDate date];
7    now =
8      [NSDate dateWithTimeIntervalSince1970: time(
           NULL)];
```

From: date.m

The **NSDate** class encapsulates an absolute time
value. This is stored as two components. One is
a well-defined fixed point: the epoch date. The
other is a time interval since that epoch.

Two standard epoch dates are supported by
NSDate, both defined in terms of the Gregorian
calendar. One is the UNIX Epoch, the first of
January, 1970. This epoch date was defined
with the first UNIX systems and was later
incorporated into the ISO C standard. The
C **time()** function will return the number of
seconds since that date.

The other Epoch time was defined as part of
the OpenStep specification, and is referred
to as the *reference date*. This one is a little
bit less arbitrary; it is the start of the current

millennium: the first day of 2001.

Part of the point of **NSDate** is to free you
from having to know which reference date
you are using. You can compare two dates
using **-compare:** or any of the related methods
irrespective of what epoch they are using
internally.

If you create a new date with **+alloc/-init**
or with **+date**, it will be set to the current
time. Dates are mutable objects, but it's
generally better to treat them as if they are not.
There is only one method for modifying dates:
-addTimeInterval:. This is deprecated in OS
X 10.6 and can cause problems in older code,
because a lot of people tend to forget that it's
possible to modify dates and just retain them,
rather than copying them.

Converting Dates for Display

```
 6   NSDate *now = [NSDate date];
 7   NSCalendar *cal = [NSCalendar currentCalendar];
 8
 9   unsigned int components = NSYearCalendarUnit;
10   NSInteger year =
11     [[cal components: components
12           fromDate: now] year];
13
14   NSString *date = [NSDateFormatter
15     localizedStringFromDate: now
16                   dateStyle:
17         NSDateFormatterLongStyle
18                   timeStyle:
19         NSDateFormatterNoStyle];
```

From: calendar.m

An **NSDate** stores an absolute time, but your
users would probably object if you presented
them with the number of seconds since 1970-01-
01 or 2001-01-01. Unless, of course, your target
market is robots.

Most of the western world standardized on the
Gregorian calendar at some point over the last
few hundred years. The earliest adopters, who
presumably got to experience all of the bugs,
included Spain, Portugal, and Italy in 1582. The
most recent was China, in 1929.

This causes some significant problems for
localization. If you have a date that represents
the 120 years before the UNIX epoch, how do
you display it? It would be the first of January,
1850 in the Gregorian calendar, but what

happens if your user's locale is a country that didn't adopt the Gregorian calendar until after this date?

A concrete example of this is the October Revolution in Russia, which took place on the seventh of November, 1917. If you present this date to Russian users, it will be incorrect, because Russia was still using the Julian calendar at this point, which is why they call something that happened in November the October Revolution.

Other locales may not use the Gregorian calendar at all. Most people who own computers probably have some experience with the Gregorian calendar, but forcing your users to perform the conversion themselves is not a good idea.

Note: The NSCalendarDate was the older OpenStep way of representing dates for display. This class is now deprecated. Unlike an NSDate, which stored an abstract time, an NSCalendarDate stored a date in the Gregorian calendar.

You might need to use one of two classes when converting a date for display. If you need to get at the individual components of the date in a particular calendar, you need to use the **NSCalendar** class. If you want to generate a string value, you should use **NSDateFormatter** instead.

The NSCalendar class encapsulates a calendar, a way of mapping between absolute times and segmented time periods containing numbered years, months, and so on. You use this class to create an NSDateComponents object from an NSDate. The NSDateComponents object encapsulates the components of a date with respect to a particular calendar.

The date components object does not store the calendar that it is relative to, and so there is no defined way of comparing two date components objects. This is intentional. If you are comparing dates, you should compare absolute times using NSDate objects and only localize them for display. This is a significant change from NSCalendarDate, which was a subclass of NSDate, so did define comparisons.

If you have a date components object, you can then construct a date for display using NSString's +stringWithFormat:. This is a bad idea. If you generate a date such as 1/2/2012, people in the USA, who use middle-endian format dates, will interpret this as the second of January, while the rest of the world, which uses little-endian dates, will read it as the first of February.

The NSDateFormatter class solves this problem for you. It has a convenient class method, +localizedStringFromDate:dateStyle:timeStyle:, that returns a string containing the localized date and time. The second and third arguments describe the level of detail required for the date and time components, respectively. This can range from not displaying anything, through a very terse numeric description, to a long description with the month and day name written out in full.

Calculating Elapsed Time

```
6    NSDate *start = [NSDate date];
7    sleep(1);
8    NSTimeInterval elapsed =
9      0 - [start timeIntervalSinceNow];
```

From: elapsed.m

You can find the difference between two date objects by sending one a -timeIntervalSinceDate: message with the other as the argument. Alternatively, to find how long ago a date was, you can send it a -timeIntervalSinceNow message. This will give a negative number if the date is in the past, so to find out how much time has elapsed since a date was created with +date or +new, you should subtract this value from zero.

This is not the fastest way of calculating the elapsed time. The **gettimeofday()** system call will return the system time in a structure. This avoids the cost of creating an object and of sending the message, but it's a bit more

work because you need to handle the structure
yourself. This structure stores the number of
seconds and microseconds in separate fields,
so the subtraction is more effort than just
comparing two scalar values.

Parsing Dates from Strings

```
6   NSDate *isoDate =
7     [NSDate dateWithString:
8       @"1982-06-15 06:10:00 +0000"];
9
10  NSLocale *gb = [[NSLocale alloc]
11    initWithLocaleIdentifier:@"en_GB"];
12  NSDateFormatter *formatter =
13    [NSDateFormatter new];
14  [formatter setLocale: gb];
15  [formatter setDateStyle:
16    NSDateFormatterShortStyle];
17  [formatter setTimeStyle:
18    NSDateFormatterNoStyle];
19  NSDate *britishDate =
20    [formatter dateFromString:
21      @"15/06/1982"];
```

From: stringdate.m

The NSDate class has a constructor that lets you construct dates from ISO 8601–formatted strings. This is useful when you are parsing dates from files used for interchange, but is not so useful when dealing with user-provided data.

If you want to create a date from a localized string, you need to return to the NSDateFormatter class. This class encapsulates some description of date formats and can perform bidirectional conversions between date and string objects.

When you create a date formatter, you can set the locale either to an explicit locale, or leave it set to the user's current locale. You can then either use one of the standard time and date formats for that locale, or specify one explicitly with the `-setDateFormat:` method. This takes a template string as an argument, but its use is discouraged in most code because it does not account for the locale.

You have one final option for reading dates. If you want to read dates from some custom format, you can use **NSScanner** to read the components from the string, then construct an **NSDateComponents** object and pass this to **NSCalendar** to create the date. **NSScanner** is covered in Chapter 5.

Receiving Timer Events

```
6   - (void)periodic: (NSTimer*)theTimer
7   {
8     NSLog(@"Timer fired");
9   }
10  - (void)start
11  {
12    SEL sel = @selector(periodic:);
13    [NSTimer scheduledTimerWithTimeInterval: 1
14                             target: self
15                           selector: sel
16                           userInfo: nil
17                            repeats: YES];
18    [[NSRunLoop currentRunLoop] run];
19  }
```

From: timer.m

The **NSTimer** class encapsulates an event source that generates events at a specific time. This is similar in principle to the **alarm()** system call, although you can have several timers scheduled at once.

You will almost always construct timers using the method from the example at the start of this section. This method will create and schedule a new timer in the same operation.

When the time interval elapses, the timer will fire. It will then send a message to an object. The simplest way of defining this message is by passing a selector, a target, and a dictionary when you create the timer. The selector must be for a method that takes one argument: an **NSTimer** instance. You can retrieve the dictionary by sending a **-userInfo** message to the timer.

There is another constructor that takes an **NSInvocation** as the argument. This is more difficult to use, but is more powerful because it allows any message with any arguments to be used.

The timer object will be autoreleased when you create it like this, but it will be retained by the *run loop* object. You can only use timers when you are using **NSRunLoop**. The run loop object sits waiting for events from the kernel— for example, timers or data becoming available on file descriptors—and then sends messages in response to these events.

If you are using AppKit or UIKit, you will be using a run loop automatically. The

NSApplication and UIApplication classes both
create a run loop instance internally. These
classes register with the run loop to receive
notifications of user interface events from the
display server and then pass them on to windows
and so on.

If you are writing a command-line application
or a server, you can still use NSRunLoop. It is
part of the Foundation framework, but you must
create it manually and tell it to run. This is very
simple, and is done in the last line of the -start
method in the preceding example.

Working with Property Lists

Property lists are a way of storing structured data. You can store two of the standard Foundation collection classes (arrays and dictionaries) in property lists, as well as most of the data types, such as strings, numbers, dates, and so on.

Property lists are intended to be abstract. They are not tied to a particular language or to a particular representation. There are currently three defined serializations for property lists. The oldest is the OpenStep property list format. This is a very dense, human-readable format.

Unfortunately, OS X cannot write the old-style property lists. It can read them, but the specification does not define a way of storing dates, or a few other things, so writing to them does not work. GNUstep extended the OpenStep property list format to allow you to store everything that the newer formats support.

With OS X, Apple introduced an XML and a binary property list format. The XML format is incredibly verbose, but has the advantage that it can be parsed by other XML-compatible tools and can be embedded in other XML documents.

The binary representation is very fast to parse and very dense but, being binary, is not human-readable.

Some libraries for other languages can handle property lists. The WINGS library in WindowMaker can read and write them, as can a library included with NetBSD. Apple's Core Foundation framework, and their open-source CFLite library, can also use them from C code.

Storing Collections in Property Lists

```
6   NSArray *array = [NSArray arrayWithObjects:
7     @"array", @"containing", @"string",
8     @"objects", nil];
9   [array writeToFile: @"example.plist" atomically:
        NO];
10  NSMutableArray *cycle = [array mutableCopy];
11  [cycle addObject: cycle];
12  [cycle writeToFile: @"failure.plist" atomically:
        NO];
```

From: writeplist.m

The array and dictionary classes implement a

`-writeToFile:atomically:` method. These let you trivially dump the contents of the collection in a file using the default property list format.

These methods are not magic. They will only work if the collections do not contain any types that cannot be stored in a property list.

If you pass **YES** as the second parameter, the method will ensure that the representation on disk is always consistent. It will write the property list to a temporary file and will then rename this file when the writing is finished.

Running the code from the start of this section will generate an example.plist file that contains an array as the root element and four strings inside it.

```
1  <?xml version="1.0" encoding="UTF-8"?>
2  <!DOCTYPE plist PUBLIC "-//Apple//DTD PLIST 1.0//
       EN" "http://www.apple.com/DTDs/PropertyList
       -1.0.dtd">
3  <plist version="1.0">
4  <array>
5    <string>array</string>
6    <string>containing</string>
7    <string>string</string>
8    <string>objects</string>
9  </array>
10 </plist>
```

From: example.plist

With current versions of OS X, this approach will use the XML property list format. As you can see, this is quite verbose. The older

OpenStep property list format used brackets for arrays and double quotes for strings, so it would have been a bit less than half the size. Converting this to the binary format reduces the file size from 294 bytes to 82.

For a property list this small, the space reduction is irrelevant. Both formats are likely to fit into a single allocation unit on disk, so they will take the same amount of on-disk space. The parsing time will be trivial for both.

This is not true with larger property lists, however. Safari, for example, stores your history in a binary property list. At the moment, mine is 15MB. If I convert it to the XML format, it becomes 34MB. The parsing overhead also increases, both in terms of CPU time and memory usage.

Unfortunately, the collection classes won't write out property list versions of themselves in anything other than the default (XML) format. Instead, you must use the `NSPropertyListSerialization` class, which we'll look at over the next few sections.

The property list formats are all hierarchical. They do not support writing cyclical data structures. The second array in this example contains a pointer to itself. The behavior when writing this to a property list is undefined. On OS X, only the elements before the recursive pointer are stored in the file. Any objects appearing after it are ignored.

Reading Data from Property Lists

```
6    NSArray *array =
7      [NSArray arrayWithContentsOfFile:
8        @"example.plist"];
9    NSData *data = [NSData dataWithContentsOfFile:
10     @"example.plist"];
11   NSMutableArray *mutable =
12     [NSPropertyListSerialization
13       propertyListFromData: data
14            mutabilityOption:
15     NSPropertyListMutableContainersAndLeaves
16                    format: NULL
17          errorDescription: NULL];
18   NSCAssert([mutable isKindOfClass:
19     [NSMutableArray class]],
20     @"Should have read a mutable array");
21   [[mutable objectAtIndex: 0]
22     appendString: @"suffix"];
```

From: readplist.m

There are two ways of reading in a property list. The first is to use the inverse of the method that we just looked at for writing them. Both of the collection classes that support property list serialization have an -initWithContentsOfFile: initializer, as well as a corresponding constructor.

This sounds easy, but there are some complications. The most important one is that property lists do not store any information about mutability. An NSString and an NSMutableString, for example, are stored in exactly the same way.

When you read back a property list, which should you get? If you read back an array by sending an **+arrayWithContentsOfFile:** message to the **NSArray** class, you get an immutable array. If you send the same message to an **NSMutableArray**, you will get a mutable array.

That's fine for the outer element in the property list, but what about the objects inside the array? In both of these cases, you will get arrays filled with immutable objects. This may not be what you want.

If you want to read back mutable objects, you need to use **NSPropertyListSerialization**. This class handles reading and writing property lists and provides much finer-grained control than the various collection classes.

Note: If you read the latest version of Apple's documentation, you will see that the method we use on NSPropertyListSerialization is marked for future deprecation. This is because it was introduced in the period when Apple started using error: parameters, but before they introduced the NSError class. Unfortunately, the method that is recommended to replace it does not yet provide equivalent functionality.

When you read a property list using this class, you can pass a mutability option as a parameter.

There are three possible options for this. The default is for all of the objects to be immutable. The option used in the example at the start of this chapter goes to the other extreme, making everything mutable. Appending a suffix to one of the strings in the array demonstrates this.

The third option is somewhere in the middle. It makes container objects mutable, but other objects (strings, numbers, dates, and so on) immutable. This is useful when you want to modify the structure of the property list but not any of the leaf elements.

When you read a property list in this way, the property list serialization class will tell you what the format of the property list was.

Converting Property List Formats

```
7    NSString *file =
8      [NSString stringWithUTF8String: argv[1]];
9    NSData *data = [NSData dataWithContentsOfFile:
10     file];
11   NSPropertyListFormat fmt;
12   id plist = [NSPropertyListSerialization
13     propertyListWithData: data
14                   options: 0
15                    format: &fmt
16                     error: NULL];
17   if (fmt == NSPropertyListBinaryFormat_v1_0)
18   {
19     return 0;
20   }
21   data = [NSPropertyListSerialization
22     dataWithPropertyList: plist
23                   format:
                             NSPropertyListBinaryFormat_v1

24                  options: 0
25                    error: NULL];
26
27   [data writeToFile: file atomically: NO];
```

From: makebinaryplist.m

On OS X, you cannot write property lists in the OpenStep format, but you can still use the two other forms. In general, you should use the binary format for storing private data and the XML format for anything that the user might want to edit with other tools.

These are not hard-and-fast rules. The point of

the property list format is that you can losslessly convert between the representations, so you might use the binary format everywhere—because it is denser and faster to parse—and expect the user to convert the property list if he wants to modify them.

You can choose which format you use when you write a file using `NSPropertyListSerialization`. This class also, helpfully, tells you what the format of the property list is currently when you read it in.

Note: The methods used in the example at the start of this section were introduced with OS X 10.6. If you are using an older version of OS X, you can replace the read method that we looked at in the last section and the corresponding write method.

It's quite common to want to store property lists in binary format for efficiency. Your users will then decide that they want to poke these files in a text editor, so they'll use the **plutil** tool to convert them to XML format. They will then, of course, forget to convert them back, so your program will read them back slowly the next time.

If you are not going to modify a property list every time your program runs, it's worth checking whether the format is still binary when you load it and then rewriting it in this format if it isn't.

Using JSON

```
22   NSData *jsonData =
23     [json dataUsingEncoding: NSUTF8StringEncoding];
24   NSError *e;
25   id object =
26     [NSJSONSerialization JSONObjectWithData:
           jsonData
27                                     options: 0
28                                     error: &e];
29   NSCAssert(nil == e, @"Failed to parse JSON");
30   NSData *data =
31     [NSJSONSerialization dataWithJSONObject: object
32                                     options:
                                       NSJSONWriti
33                                     error: &e];
34   NSCAssert(nil == e, @"Failed to export JSON");
```

From: json.m

Over the last few years, another format that is very similar to the old-style OpenStep property lists has become popular. The *JavaScript Object Notation (JSON)* is a subset of serialized JavaScript objects, storing data but not code.

Recent versions of Cocoa include a class modeled on **NSPropertyListSerialization** for loading and storing JSON data. This has slightly more restrictions than the property list encoding. You can only store numbers or strings in leaf nodes, and all collections must be arrays or dictionaries.

In general, you wouldn't use JSON for applications that live in a pure Objective-C environment. JSON is mainly useful for interoperability. There are libraries available for most platforms and languages that read and write JSON and it's the native format for most web applications. If you write JSON data, it's trivial for a piece of client-side JavaScript on a web page to transform it. The same is true in reverse: You can generate JSON on a web page and then use it in your Objective-C code.

The example at the start of this section shows how to convert to and from JSON. The JSON standard requires data to be in some unicode encoding. The serialization class can automatically detect the encoding, because the first two characters in a JSON stream are always ASCII. This lets it detect multibyte encodings by the placement of NULL bytes within the first four, if a byte-order mark is missing.

In this example, we pretty-print the JSON. This is mostly useful for debugging. It will automatically indent the output, for readability. This takes a tiny bit more CPU and can use a lot more space, so it's a bad idea for data that's going to go across the network and be used by another program, but a good idea if the data is going to be edited by hand.

Storing User Defaults

```
6    NSUserDefaults *def =
7      [NSUserDefaults standardUserDefaults];
8    id persistentString =
9      [def stringForKey: @"example"];
10   NSLog(@"Old value: %@", persistentString);
11   if (argc > 1)
12   {
13     NSString *new =
14       [NSString stringWithUTF8String:
15         argv[1]];
16     [def setObject: new
17            forKey: @"example"];
18     [def synchronize];
19   }
```

From: defaults.m

The user defaults system is one of the biggest
users of property lists. If you look in the
~/Library/Preferences directory, you will see a lot
of property list files. These files store preferences
for the current user. There is a corresponding
global directory in /Library/Preferences.

Every application has its own *defaults domain*,
typically a reverse-DNS notation string
(for example com.apple.TextEdit). The
NSUserDefaults class can access data from this
domain.

The user defaults system will read data from
a variety of sources. One of the most useful is
the command line. You can specify key-value
pairs as command-line arguments to any OS
X application, which is incredibly useful when

debugging.

The defaults system is exposed as a single dictionary, with a few convenience methods. In general, you can pretend that the user defaults object really is a persistent dictionary.

Note: The defaults system is comparable to the Windows registry, but with a few important differences. Both support multiple levels of keys (user, system, and network), but the defaults system hides all of this from the programmer. Although both look like tree structures, the registry is a single database, whereas the defaults system stores data in separate files for each domain. This makes it easy to modify defaults with third-party tools and means that it scales better because you never need to read more than one or two of these files into memory at once. The downside is that operations on defaults are not transactional. Modifying the same domain from two programs simultaneously is undefined.

Unlike a dictionary, the defaults object has some convenience methods for accessing non-object types and for type-checking object types. In the current example, we send it a **–stringForKey:** message. This wraps the **–objectForKey:** method, but ensures that the return value is a string.

There are other convenience methods, such as **–floatForKey:** and **–setFloat:ForKey:**,

which take primitive C types and wrap them in
`NSNumber` instances before storing them in the
defaults system.

The code in this example ends by sending a
`-synchronize` message to the defaults object.
This is not usually necessary. The defaults
object will be periodically synchronized with the
on-disk storage. In this example, however, we are
not using a run loop (so timers will not work)
and are exiting immediately after modifying the
defaults, so our changes will never be committed
to disk without this.

Running this example, you can see that the
initial value is `nil`, because there isn't anything
stored in defaults. The value passed as an
argument to the short program is stored in
defaults and retrieved automatically the next
time it is run.

This also demonstrates using `NSArgumentDomain`.
There are several sources for defaults, which are
loaded in order and overwrite the previous ones.
The last, and therefore highest priority, defaults
are the arguments. Specifying an -example
command-line option sets the `@"example"` key in
defaults to whatever is passed as the argument.

This does not replace the persistent value, it just
overrides it in this particular run of the program.
You can see that when we run the program
again, without the command-line argument, the
old value from two invocations ago is used. This
was committed to disk on the third run of the

```
1  $ ./a.out persistent
2  a.out[72216:903] Old value: (nil)
3  $ ./a.out new
4  a.out[72216:903] Old value: persistent
5  $ ./a.out -example arg store
6  a.out[72362:903] Old value: arg
7  $ ./a.out -example arg
8  a.out[72363:903] Old value: arg
9  $ ./a.out new
10 a.out[72363:903] Old value: store
11 $ plutil -convert xml1 \
12   ~/Library/Preferences/a.out.plist
13 $ cat ~/Library/Preferences/a.out.plist
14 <?xml version="1.0" encoding="UTF-8"?>
15 <!DOCTYPE plist PUBLIC "-//Apple//DTD PLIST 1.0//
       EN" "http://www.apple.com/DTDs/PropertyList
       -1.0.dtd">
16 <plist version="1.0">
17 <dict>
18   <key>example</key>
19   <string>new</string>
20 </dict>
21 </plist>
```

Output from: defaults

program, but was not used on the fourth run
because an argument replaced it. On the fifth
run, with no -example argument, it is visible
again. You can look in individual domains
explicitly with NSUserDefaults, but it's rare
to want to.

If you are writing a command-line tool, this
provides a very convenient way of parsing
command-line arguments. You can store default

values for command-line arguments in the
defaults system and have them automatically
overridden by the user, without needing any
parsing code.

Storing Arbitrary Objects in User Defaults

```
 6    NSUserDefaults *def =
 7      [NSUserDefaults standardUserDefaults];
 8    NSData *serialized = [def objectForKey: @"color"
          ];
 9
10    id favoriteColor =
11      [NSKeyedUnarchiver unarchiveObjectWithData:
12        serialized];
13
14    if (nil == favoriteColor)
15    {
16      favoriteColor = [NSColor blackColor];
17      serialized = [NSKeyedArchiver
18        archivedDataWithRootObject: favoriteColor];
19      [def setObject: serialized
20              forKey: @"color"];
21      [def synchronize];
22    }
```

From: colordefault.m

Quite often, you want to store something in
defaults other than the basic Foundation data
types. A common example is colors. If you allow
users to customize the interface in any way, you
typically want their selected colors to persist
between program invocations. This is easy; just

store the `NSColor` object in defaults.

Well, it would be easy if property lists and, by extension, user defaults supported `NSColor` objects. Unfortunately, they don't. You can, however, store `NSData` instances in defaults. If you have some mechanism for turning an object into data, you can store it in defaults.

Fortunately, there is a generic way that a lot of common objects support. Any object that implements the `NSCoding` protocol can be serialized and deserialized using an `NSCoder` subclass.

Unlike property lists, the `NSCoder` mechanism supports arbitrary objects and cycles. Unfortunately, it requires the object to implement the two methods in the `NSCoding` protocol, so it doesn't work on all objects. It does work on a lot, however, and it's trivial to reuse for storing objects in defaults.

If you are doing this a lot, it's very easy to write a *category* on `NSUserDefaults` that adds `-colorForKey:` and `-setColor:forKey:` methods. These can take an `NSColor` instance, serialize it with a coder, and then restore it.

If you want an even more general solution, you could add a `-setEncodedObject:forKey:` method. This would take an **id**`<NSCoding>` as its argument and store it using the code from the example at the start of this chapter.

If you want to store some object that doesn't support the `NSCoding` protocol in defaults, you

have two options. First, you can add `NSCoding`
support to it. This involves implementing the
`-encodeWithCoder:` and `-initWithCoder:`
methods, which you can do in a category.

The second is to do some other kind
of transformation. A lot of object have
`-stringValue` and `-initWithString:` methods.
You can store these in defaults simply by turning
them into strings before storing them and
creating new objects from strings when you read
them from defaults.

10

Interacting with the Environment

Objective-C is generally used on UNIX-like platforms, and it inherits the notion of an environment from there. This includes concepts such as a working directory, environment variables, and so on.

In a traditional Objective-C environment, you were expected to get these values in exactly the same way you would from a C program. With OpenStep, Sun and NeXT introduced the NSProcessInfo class, which provides a higher level of abstraction.

Part of the motivation for this was the fact OpenStep programs were expected to run on OPENSTEP, Solaris, and Windows NT. All of these have subtle differences in their idea of an environment, and some abstraction was required to hide them.

Getting Environment Variables

```objc
3   int main(int argc, char **argv, char **envp)
4   {
5     // The C way
6     while (*envp)
7     {
8       printf("%s\n", *envp);
9       envp++;
10    }
11    printf("Working Directory: %s\n", getenv("PWD")
          );
12
13    // The Objective-C way
14    [NSAutoreleasePool new];
15    NSDictionary *env =
16      [[NSProcessInfo processInfo] environment];
17    for (NSString *key in env)
18    {
19      NSLog(@"%@ = %@", key, [env objectForKey: key
            ]);
20    }
21    NSLog(@"Working Directory: %@\n",
22        [env objectForKey: @"PWD"]);
23    return 0;
24  }
```

From: env.m

Environment variables can be accessed in three ways on OS X. Two of them will work anywhere, whereas the third will only work on some platforms.

OS X, like Windows and a lot of UNIX systems, passes the environment into processes as a third argument to the **main()** function. This is a **NULL**-terminated C array of C strings. The C and POSIX standards don't require this third argument to work, so it's a bad idea to rely on it in portable code.

When a program starts, the run time loader will load all required shared libraries and then jump to a special function in the C standard library, typically called `_start`. This then calls `main()`, but before it does it stores a pointer to the environment variables.

You can access this storage by calling the `getenv()` C standard function. Alternatively, you can access environment variables by sending an `-environment` message to the singleton process info object. This returns a dictionary containing the environment.

Note: There is no way of setting environment variables using Objective-C code. Modifying the environment is typically done in C code as a preliminary to calling one of the `exec()` family of functions. This only works on UNIX-like platforms and not, for example, on Windows or Symbian systems. Therefore, it is discouraged. You can set a new dictionary that will be used as the environment of a new child process by sending a `-setEnvironment:` message to NSTask.

Parsing Command-Line Arguments

```
3    int main(int argc, char **argv)
4    {
5      [NSAutoreleasePool new];
6      NSUserDefaults *d =
7        [NSUserDefaults standardUserDefaults];
8      NSString *file = [d stringForKey: @"file"];
9      if (nil == file)
10     {
11       fprintf(stderr,
12         "USAGE: %s -file {filename}", argv[0]);
13       return 1;
14     }
15     NSLog(@"Using file %@", file);
16     return 0;
17   }
```

From: args.m

Standard C does not provide a way of getting at program arguments outside of the main() function. The GNU C standard library provides some extensions for accessing them after program start, and on most UNIX-like platforms you can read them from the /proc filesystem, but there's no simple way of getting them in a portable way from C code.

With Objective-C, you can always get at the arguments by sending an -arguments message to NSProcessInfo. This returns an NSArray containing Objective-C strings for all of the options. You can then process the arguments in any way you like.

It's quite unusual to access arguments this way. The simplest way of parsing command-line arguments, as we saw in the last chapter, is to use the `NSArgumentDomain` in `NSUserDefaults`. When an Objective-C program is started, the command-line arguments are all read and inserted into a dictionary, which is used by the defaults system.

This makes it very easy to provide a set of command-line arguments along with (configurable) default values. You never interact with the arguments directly when you use this approach. Instead, you ask the defaults system for a value for a key, and it returns something that may be from a persistent storage location or from the command line.

In the EtoileFoundation framework, we provide an `ETGetOptionsDictionary()` function, which wraps the standard `getopt()` function. This provides an Objective-C way of using UNIX-style command-line arguments. You can use this if you are writing a UNIX-style tool in Objective-C. Otherwise, it is better to use the defaults system.

Accessing the User's Locale

```
  6    NSLocale *l =
  7      [NSLocale autoupdatingCurrentLocale];
  8    NSString *language =
  9      [l objectForKey: NSLocaleIdentifier];
 10    NSString *humanReadableLanguage =
 11      [l displayNameForKey: NSLocaleIdentifier
 12                     value: language];
```

From: locale.m

If your program interacts with the user directly in any way, you will probably want to localize it at some point. Objective-C provides a lot of rich facilities for doing this.

The NSLocale object encapsulates a locale. There are several ways of getting instances of this class. If you send it a +systemLocale message, you will get the system locale. However, this is not something you should normally use. It is the fallback locale for when the user's locale does not work correctly.

You can get the user's current locale in two ways. Sending a +currentLocale message returns a locale object that encapsulates the current locale. If the user selects a new locale, a NSCurrentLocaleDidChangeNotification will be posted, and you can get a new locale object for the new locale.

Alternatively, you can send an +autoupdatingCurrentLocale message to the class. This returns a locale object that will always represent the current locale, even if it changes. This can be slightly confusing because two subsequent calls to the same method with the same argument on this object might return different values.

It is important to avoid caching data returned from locale objects, if you want to support changing locale while the program is running. If you are presenting things to the user that remain on the screen, you should make sure that you monitor the notification and update them, even if you are using an autoupdating locale object.

Supporting Sudden Termination

```
11  NSProcessInfo *p =
12    [NSProcessInfo processInfo];
13  [p enableSuddenTermination];
14  // Do initialization
15  [p disableSuddenTermination];
16  // Do other things that can't
17  // be interrupted here.
18  modifyFiles();
19  [p enableSuddenTermination];
```

From: suddenDeath.m

Traditionally, there are two options for process termination. A process can exit gracefully, by reaching a safe place to stop and then calling **exit()** or reaching the **return** statement in the **main()** function. Alternatively, it can exit abruptly, by receiving an unhandled signal, including something like a segmentation fault.

In both cases, the kernel will reclaim all of its shared resources, but in the case of abrupt termination some of these resources may have been left in an inconsistent state. A typical example of this is a file in the course of being modified.

This used to be a big problem with complex applications, such as word processors. They would open the file for writing, start modifying it, then crash, leaving the file in a state where it was very difficult to recover the contents. You can avoid this by using the atomic writing facilities on most Foundation objects, which write to a temporary file and then rename it, so the write either succeeds entirely or fails entirely—it doesn't even half succeed.

With OS X 10.6, Apple introduced the *sudden termination* mechanism. The theory behind this was that a lot of programs spend a lot of time on exit running destructors for objects that have no effects other than to release memory that the operating system will reclaim anyway. With sudden termination, a process can advertise that it doesn't have any unsaved data. The operating system is then free to kill it abruptly, rather than request that it exit gracefully.

This is particularly useful for long-running background tasks that are idle for a long time. They will generally be swapped out by the kernel. When you ask them to exit gracefully, a lot of code and data needs to be paged in to handle the exit. With sudden termination, the pages in the swap file will just be flagged as available for reuse.

Supporting sudden termination in your application is very easy. You call two methods on **NSProcessInfo**, one on either side of some action that can't be interrupted.

Note: If you use AppKit with the NSDocument infrastructure, you don't need to do anything. Your application will be marked as not supporting sudden termination when any documents have unsaved data.

These methods are called
-disableSuddenTermination and
-enableSuddenTermination, but the names are slightly misleading. They don't actually enable and disable sudden termination, they modify a counter. When the counter reaches 0, the application is marked as being killable.

This means that you can use them in different threads or nest them without any problems. The counter starts set to one, so you must explicitly send an **-enableSuddenTermination** message to the process info object to enable it. If you are creating an application, you can avoid this by setting a key in the application bundle's property list file.

Cocoa applications, as opposed to command-line tools, are typically distributed as bundles.

These are directories that should be treated
as files by graphical file managers. NeXT
used them very effectively to store binaries
for different operating systems in the same
application, allowing a file server to contain
a single application for OPENSTEP, Solaris,
and even Windows. One of the things that
this bundle contains is a property list, called
info.plist, which describes some attributes about
the application, such as the name of its principle
class, the resources to load at startup, and so
on. The initial sudden termination state is one of
these attributes.

With iOS and OS X 10.7, sudden termination is
quite important. These systems will terminate
applications using sudden termination when
they run low on memory. The applications are
expected to be able to restart without losing any
user-visible state. With OS X 10.7, each window
in the application is expected to be able to store
its state and be reloaded automatically.

11

Key-Value Coding

A lot of code in a typical program is involved with accessing and modifying aspects of an object's state.

The *key-value coding (KVC)* mechanism is intended to provide an abstract interface for setting and getting properties on objects. It is combined with the *key-value observing (KVO)* mechanism, which provides an abstract way of observing changes in a particular property of another object.

KVC lets you interact with every object as if it were a dictionary. You use the same mechanism for reading and writing properties, irrespective of how they are stored. The main advantage is that it eliminates a lot of the need to write custom controller classes to fit model objects to views.

A view class generally needs to get and set properties on a model object. With KVC, there is a generic, parameterized mechanism for doing this. You can just provide a view object with

a key or key path and have it automatically
retrieve the data from the model, without
needing to know any details of the model's
implementation, or even its interface beyond the
fact that it supports KVC.

Accessing Values by Key

```
68   [object setValue: @"42"
69           forKey: @"integer"];
70   int value =
71     [[object valueForKey: @"integer"]
72       intValue];
73   NSCAssert(value == 42,
74       @"Value set and retrieved");
```

From: kvc.m

Objects manipulated via KVC look much like
dictionaries. The NSDictionary class is, itself,
KVC compliant, although you typically don't use
the KVC methods when using it.

The two most common methods for interacting
with KVC-compliant objects are –valueForKey:
and –setValue:forKey:. The –objectForKey:
method on NSDictionary behaves in almost
the same way for retrieving values. The two
set methods on NSDictionary work slightly
differently.

The first thing you will notice is that
you get a compile-time warning if
you use –setObject:forKey: on an
immutable dictionary. You won't if you

use `-setValue:forKey:`. This method is
implemented by `NSObject`. It will fail at
run time when you call it on an immutable
dictionary, but there will be no hint of this at
compile time.

The other big difference is the use of `nil`. If you
use `nil` as the value with `-setValue:forKey:`,
it will delete that key. If you do the same for
`-setObject:forKey:`, you get an exception.

Ensuring KVC Compliance

```
3   @interface KeyPublic : NSObject @end
4   @implementation KeyPublic @end
5
6   @interface KeyIVar : KeyPublic
7   {
8      int integer;
9   }
10  @end
11  @implementation KeyIVar @end
```

From: kvc.m

When you use the KVC methods, you almost
always call the implementations in `NSObject`.
These then try to work out how the property
should really be accessed.

The first place they will look is at accessor
methods. By convention, Objective-C classes
provide `-property` and `-setProperty:` methods
for reading and setting the "property." If your
class provides these, they will be called. KVC

will also look for a few other methods, including
things such as -isProperty for a Boolean
property.

```
13   @interface KeyAccessor : KeyIVar @end
14   @implementation KeyAccessor
15   - (int)integer
16   {
17     return integer;
18   }
19   - (void)setInteger: (int)aValue
20   {
21     integer = aValue;
22   }
23   @end
24   @interface KeyProperty : KeyPublic
25   @property int integer;
26   @end
27   @implementation KeyProperty
28   @synthesize integer;
29   @end
```

From: kvc.m

If this fails, the class will be sent an
+accessInstanceVariablesDirectly message.
If this returns **YES**, the KVC methods will
look for an instance variable that matches
the name of the property and use that. The
implementation of this method in **NSObject** does
return **YES**, so you only need to override it if you
want to prevent KVC from looking at instance
variables.

Finally, if this fails, the KVC code will call
one of two fallback methods, depending on

whether you are setting or getting the property.
These are −valueForUndefinedKey: and
−setValue:forUndefinedKey:.

```objc
31   @interface KeyFallback : KeyPublic
32   {
33     NSMutableDictionary *dict;
34   }
35   @end
36   @implementation KeyFallback
37   - (id)valueForUndefinedKey: (NSString*)aKey
38   {
39     return [dict valueForKey: aKey];
40   }
41   - (void)setValue: (id)aValue
42    forUndefinedKey: (NSString*)aKey
43   {
44     [dict setValue: aValue
45            forKey: aKey];
46   }
47   @end
```

From: kvc.m

These methods are the last chance to support
KVC. If you implement them, you should call
the superclass implementation for all keys
you don't support directly. This will throw an
exception if called on the root class, indicating
that you don't properly handle the key.

If you use declared properties to synthesize
accessor methods, you will get KVC compliance
for free. The kvc.m example shows all of the
different ways in which you can implement the
same KVC property.

This example uses one public class and a number of private subclasses that all support the property. You can use instances of all of these classes interchangeably, at least when it comes to storing that key. More importantly, you can use something like the `KeyIVar` or `KeyFallback` class for prototyping and then switch to something else later.

The fallback method is especially useful when prototyping. When you start working, create a private dictionary instance variable and access all of the properties on the object via KVC. Once you've determined the properties your class really needs, you can replace the fallback implementation with a set of accessors and, as a separate step, replace the KVC calls with direct message sends.

One thing that you might have noticed about this example is that KVC only deals with objects, but the instance variable is an **int**. Somehow, this still works. This is because KVC performs *auto-boxing*. We set this property by passing @*"12"* as an argument to `-setValue:forKey:`. The KVC code sent an `-intValue` message to the string object, after finding that the property was an integer.

In the other direction, it constructed an `NSNumber` encapsulating the primitive value. If the instance variable or accessor methods use object types, this code is bypassed. Note that KVC only accesses the runtime type information and all object types are encoded as *"@"* in type encodings.

This means you can use KVC to set an **NSString** instance as the value for an instance variable declared as an **NSArray**. KVC won't generate any errors when you try this, and neither will the compiler. The receiver, however, will get an exception the next time it sends a message such as **-objectAtIndex:** to the string.

If you are writing KVC accessors for object types, you might want to add an assert statement checks whether the object has a compatible class.

Understanding Key Paths

So far, we've looked at getting and setting values for an individual key. This is quite useful, but it doesn't quite demonstrate the full flexibility of KVC.

Most of what we've used KVC for could be done quite easily without KVC. If you want one object to access a particular property of another object, and don't want to hard code it, you could just store a selector and use the normal Objective-C message-sending mechanism to call it.

This works fine if the property is stored on that object, but what happens if you want an indirect property? You could store an array of selectors, and use each one to get the intermediate object, but that is cumbersome.

With KVC, you can use *key paths*. These are simple strings containing key names, separated by dots. If you want to access a property of a property of an object, then you can do so in a single operation using key paths.

Note: The dot notation for accessing declared properties looks very similar to the KVC notation, and it's very easy to confuse the two. This is unfortunate, because they are entirely unrelated. The dot notation generates message sends to accessor methods directly. The KVC methods taking key paths are a higher-level abstraction. This is one of the reasons why the dot notation is widely disliked.

The similarity is, unfortunately, intentional. Before the public release, Apple employees were referring to declared properties using the KVC terminology, and the two were probably meant to be more closely related.

The big advantage of key paths is that a generic view object, for example, only needs to store one pointer to the model object. It doesn't need pointers to various components inside the model, it can access these via key paths.

For example, if you had a view for displaying information about a person, you could join copies in a family tree using the @"father" and @"mother" key paths. You could then use the same view in something displaying grandparent relations with the @*"father.mother"* key path, and so on.

Key paths are used a lot with *Cocoa bindings*. These are generic controller classes that connect models to views.

Observing Keys

```
5   + (void)observeValueForKeyPath:
6                    (NSString*)keyPath
7        ofObject: (id)object
8          change: (NSDictionary*)change
9         context: (void*)context
10  {
11    NSLog(@"%@.%@ is now %@", object, keyPath,
12      [change objectForKey: NSKeyValueChangeNewKey
           ]);
13  }
14  + (void)watchChange
15  {
16    NSMutableDictionary *dict =
17      [NSMutableDictionary new];
18    [dict addObserver: self
19          forKeyPath: @"aKey"
20              options:
21      NSKeyValueObservingOptionNew
22              context: NULL];
23
24    [dict setObject: @"set as object"
25            forKey: @"aKey"];
26
27    [dict removeObserver: self
28            forKeyPath: @"aKey"];
```

From: kvo.m

Having a uniform mechanism for setting and

getting keys is useful, but it's not particularly special. The real power of KVC comes from KVO, which lets you monitor keys for changes.

The bindings mechanism uses KVC and KVO to eliminate the need for controllers in a lot of cases. When a view wants to modify a model, it uses KVC. When the model changes, the view gets the notification from KVO and updates itself to reflect the change. The combination of these two—closely related—technologies allows you to have tight connections between objects without tight coupling of their designs.

Registering as a KVO observer is a lot like registering to receive notifications (see Chapter 16), but with a few differences. One of the most important is that KVO notifications are always sent to the same method. The first method in the sample code at the start of this section shows what this should look like.

In this example, it's a class method. Most of the time, you will use instance methods, but it's important to remember that classes are objects in Objective-C, so you can use them in almost any place where you'd normally use an object.

This implementation is quite simple; it just logs the new value for the key. The second method shows how to register for the notification. The **change** argument in the notification method is a dictionary, which, in this version, contains the new value for the key. It only contains the new value because that's all that we asked for.

The **options:** parameter in the method for adding the observer is a bitfield. You can request just the new value, just the old value, or both. You can also request notifications both before and after the change.

This lets you easily perform tasks such as recording the changes made to an object, which is helpful for implementing undo support. If your model objects are KVO compliant, you can get notifications of every change, save the old value, and then revert it (using KVC) later. The logic for implementing undo like this can be completely decoupled from the implementation details of your model objects.

Ensuring KVO Compliance

```
34    [self setValue: @"42"
35            forKey: @"aKey"];
36    self.aKey = 12;
37    [self willChangeValueForKey: @"aKey"];
38    aKey = 47;
39    [self didChangeValueForKey: @"aKey"];
```

From: kvo2.m

KVO, like the rest of Objective-C, is not magic. If you set a key using the KVC accessors, it's trivial for notifications to be sent to observers. What happens if you set an instance variable directly? Unfortunately, the answer is quite simple: Nothing.

Setting an instance variable directly is just a store into memory. There is no easy way of automatically detecting when a single value in memory has been modified. This means you must bracket direct accesses to instance variables with the two calls shown in the snippet at the start of this section.

These will fire off the KVO notifications, if required. Note that you do not need to send these messages if you are calling an accessor method. This is one of the advantages of the late binding that you find in Objective-C.

The code that implements KVO is quite complex and uses some of the more advanced features of Objective-C. When you register an observer for a key, the set method for that key will be replaced by a special version that will handle the notifications.

KVO is probably the part of the Foundation framework that seems the most like magic. It's worth remembering that KVO does nothing that your own code can't. It does not rely on any undocumented interfaces, compiler modifications, or similar tricks. You can implement something equivalent in your own code if you want to. You can look at the GNUstep implementation to see how this might be done.

On both GNUstep and OS X, the KVO mechanism is implemented using *isa-swizzling*. This is a trick whereby the **isa** pointer of an object is switched to point to a different class after the object's creation. Typically, this trick is combined with run-time class creation, so you insert a new class as a leaf node of the class hierarchy, and make the object's `isa` pointer point to it.

Fortunately, the point of systems such as KVO being part of the Foundation framework is to free you from needing to know exactly how they work, unless you are particularly interested. There is one important side-effect of KVO (and other things) being implemented using isa-swizzling, however. It means you should not depend on an object's `isa` pointer pointing to a specific class or being unmodified.

If you want to test whether an object is an instance of a particular class, use `-isMemberOfClass:` or `-isKindOfClass:`. Send an object a `-class` message to get its class, don't just inspect the `isa` pointer.

12

Handling Errors

Most code contains bugs. Good code is aware of this and will handle them gracefully. Really good code uses formal methods to prove that there are no bugs, but most people can't afford really good code.

Most of the sample code in this book pretends that errors never happen. This book has quite small pages, and proper error-handling code for any of the examples would fill them up very quickly with things that are largely irrelevant to the point of the example.

Most errors that can be detected at run time come from one function or method calling another with invalid inputs. The best way of handling this depends a lot on the language. For example, Erlang discourages defensive programming at the module level; if your module is in an undefined state, you should kill it and create a new version. In C, you are encouraged to validate every input and check every return value. In Java, you can defer error handling by using exceptions. Lisp and Smalltalk let you inspect the stack when an error occurs and dynamically fix the code that gave you the wrong input.

Objective-C fits somewhere between C and Java in this respect. Some errors are best handled very close to their cause, whereas others can only be handled by reporting the cause and exiting.

Objective-C has had things called *exceptions* since the NeXT days, but they've only behaved like exceptions in other languages for the last few years. As a superset of C, however, Objective-C has support for all of the forms of error reporting that you find in C.

Runtime Differences for Exceptions

Exception handling is quite difficult to implement. When you throw an exception, you need to unwind every stack frame between where the exception was thrown and where it is caught. There are a few ways of doing this. In a language with stack introspection like Smalltalk, it's relatively easy. The exception can look at each stack frame and perform the unwinding.

In Java and similar languages, it is commonly implemented by returning two values. In a typical Java VM, one register will be reserved for returning the exception object. After every call, the JVM will check that this register is zero, and branch to the exception-handling code if it isn't.

This is not possible in Objective-C, because you need to be able to interoperate with C. Some of the stack frames between where the exception is thrown and where it is caught might be C, and you can't expect all C code on the system to be modified to return another value if an exception is thrown.

Another option is something like Microsoft's *structured exception handling (SEH)*, where a linked list of cleanup code addresses is pushed and popped as exception-handling blocks are entered and left. When an exception is thrown, this stack is used to find the cleanup code to run and to jump to the correct location in the stack. This would have been an option for Objective-C, but it's quite expensive. It requires you to run some code whenever you enter and exit an exception-handling block, then some more when you throw an exception.

C does include a pair of calls that let you do something like stack unwinding, though. The `setjmp()` call stores the current CPU registers, including the stack and frame pointers. The `longjmp()` call reloads them. This has the effect of resetting the stack to the state when `setjmp()` was called. This is how Objective-C exceptions were traditionally implemented.

As you can imagine, this was far from ideal.

There was no support for performing cleanup actions in intervening stack frames. If your Objective-C code called some C++ code, which then called Objective-C code again, you could `longjmp()` over the C++ code, preventing it from running destructors.

The GNU runtime got C++-compatible exception handling back in 2004. Every function compiled in this mode, irrespective of the source language, had some DWARF debugging data exported describing the layout of the stack frame and how to unwind it. This is often called *zero-cost exception handling* because it doesn't impose any run-time penalty on code that doesn't use exception handling. If you compile C code in this mode, the binary is a bit bigger from the extra unwinding information, but this extra data isn't even swapped in unless an exception is thrown through the C code.

With this support, it was possible to run cleanup code in C++ when an Objective-C exception was thrown through C++ stack frames, and vice versa. It's also possible to register cleanup code in C, using the `__attribute__((cleanup))` GCC extension.

Apple adopted this change with the 64-bit runtime. This changed the performance characteristics of exceptions quite significantly. With `setjmp()`/`longjmp()` exceptions, entering an exception-handling region was expensive (it required saving all registers) but throwing an exception was quite fast. It was, however, also unsafe, so the documentation recommended that catching an exception should usually be followed by aborting the program. Exceptions were to be used for semi-graceful abnormal termination, unless they were caught very close to where they were thrown.

With zero-cost exceptions, it costs nothing to enter an exception-handling block. Throwing an exception is very expensive, but safe. This means that you can put **@try** blocks in your code without slowing anything down and throw exceptions whenever something exceptional happens.

If you need compatibility with Apple's 32-bit runtime, it's still a good idea to avoid exceptions; they will add a lot of overhead if you frequently use **@try** blocks.

Note: When using the older-style exceptions, you must be careful to specify **volatile** for any local variables you need to access after catching the exception. If you don't, they may be restored to the value they held when setjmp() was called.

Throwing and Catching Exceptions

```
6    NSArray *array = [NSArray array];
7    @try
8    {
9      [array objectAtIndex: 0];
10   }
11   @catch (NSException *e)
12   {
13     NSLog(@"Caught exception %@", e);
14   }
```

From: exception.m

Old Objective-C code is likely to contain blocks that start NS_DURING. These are the old macros that defined the setjmp()-style exception handling. With newer versions of the Foundation framework, they are defined in NSException.h to use the new exception-handling keywords.

These old macros have a couple of limitations, even when they are being used as wrappers around the new keywords. First, they only allow NSException instances to be caught. Second, they have no equivalent of **@finally**, which runs cleanup code and then continues unwinding, although you can simulate this by catching an exception and then rethrowing it.

These macros were quite inconvenient to use. You were required to use NS_VALUERETURN or NS_VOIDRETURN to return from inside an NS_DURING block, to make sure that you removed the cleanup code from the exception-handling stack.

```
67  #define NS_DURING      @try {
68  #define NS_HANDLER     } @catch (NSException *
        localException) {
69  #define NS_ENDHANDLER  }
70  #define NS_VALUERETURN(v,t) return (v)
71  #define NS_VOIDRETURN   return
```

From: NSException.h

Now, exception-handling code looks a lot like Java or C++. There are a few restrictions. Throwing objects other than **NSException** may work, but it's unsupported. On OS X, this is because an object thrown when compiled with the legacy runtime may still be caught with the old **NS_HANDLER** macro, which expects an **NSException** instance. With the GCC runtime (but not the GNUstep runtime), it is possible to throw an instance of a class that has not been registered properly with the runtime, causing a crash in the unwinding library. Throwing non-object types is not supported at all.

The best way of throwing an exception is still to send a **-raise** message to an NSException instance. You may also use the **@throw** keyword to throw an arbitrary object, but don't be too surprised if it doesn't work. If you are using the GNU runtime or the modern Apple runtime it probably will work, but you're doing something that isn't well tested.

Using Exception Objects

```
5    [NSException raise: NSGenericException
6        format: @"This is an example"];
```

From: throwexception.m

The **NSException** class used to implement a stack of **longjmp()** buffers and jump to the top one on the stack when required. Now, the unwinding is all done by the runtime and unwinding libraries, but **NSException** is still used to encapsulate exceptions.

Exceptions have three components: a name, a reason, and a user info dictionary. The name is a unique identifier for this type of exception. This is just a string, but it is common to use a symbolic constant, such as **NSRangeException**, so that you can do a pointer comparison on the exception name when you catch an exception.

The description is a human-readable description. This is generally only used for debugging, so localization isn't important. It's more important that you understand what happened than that your users do. Finally, the user info dictionary is an **NSDictionary** containing some key-value pairs. It's entirely up to the code throwing the exception to decide what goes in here, although most exception-throwing methods document what they will put in their user info dictionaries.

You can use this for passing arbitrary information up to wherever the exception is caught. Because it is a dictionary, you can decide to add some extra keys later without breaking binary compatibility with existing code.

This is one of the cases where it's common to use an immutable dictionary—an `NSDictionary`, rather than an `NSMutableDictionary`—because the catching code does not expect to be able to modify it. You will often use `NSDictionary`'s `+dictionaryWithValuesAndKeys:` constructor to create a single-use immutable dictionary to throw, if you are attaching a dictionary to the exception.

On recent versions of OS X, the exception object also has some extra information that is useful for debugging. Sending it a `-callStackReturnAddresses` message will give you an `NSArray` containing `NSNumber`s pointing to the return addresses of all of the functions on the stack. This is not particularly useful, but the `-callStackSymbols` method, introduced with OS X 10.6, is. It gives you the names of all of the functions or methods on the stack when the exception was created.

This latter method is used by the unhandled exception handler, which is called whenever unwinding an exception is not caught, to print a stack trace before the program aborts. You may want to use the `NSSetUncaughtExceptionHandler()` function to replace this handler with something of your own. If you have an error reporting mechanism, then having the back trace from an unhandled exception can be very useful.

Using the Unified Exception Model

```
5    try {
6      @throw @"An exception!";
7    } catch (int a) {
8      NSLog(@"Caught: %d", a);
9    } catch (id exception) {
10     NSLog(@"Caught: %@", exception);
11   }
```

From: tryCatch.mm

With early Objective-C++ implementations, the Objective-C and C++ exception models were completely different and incompatible. You could throw C++ exceptions with **throw** and catch them with **catch**. You could throw Objective-C++ exceptions with **@throw** and catch them with **@catch**. You could mix these two within a program, but not within the same function and not for the same exception.

With more recent implementations, Objective-C++ uses a unified exception model. A **catch** statement with an Objective-C type can catch objects thrown with **@throw**. Similarly, a **throw** statement with an Objective-C type produces an exception that can be caught with **@catch**.

The snippet at the start of this section shows

this in operation, in a trivial case. This will be rejected by old Objective-C++ compilers. You can use this to check whether your target supports the unified exception model.

Managing Memory with Exceptions

```
12   id pool = [NSAutoreleasePool new];
13   id array = [NSArray new];
14   @try
15   {
16     throw(array);
17   }
18   @catch (id e)
19   {
20     NSLog(@"Caught exception %@", e);
21     e = [e retain];
22     [pool drain];
23     [e autorelease];
24     pool = nil;
25     @throw;
26   }
27   @finally
28   {
29     [array release];
30     [pool drain];
31   }
```

From: releaseexcept.m

Exception handling makes memory management a bit more difficult. If you create a new object in a method and then release it at the end, you must take into account the fact that exceptions are a thinly disguised non-local goto and that there are suddenly lots of ways to return from your method. Every single function call or message send becomes a potential return path.

You can fix this quite easily by adding an **@finally** block at the end of the **@try** block. Code in this block will always be executed, whether you exit the **@try** block by reaching the end or by throwing an exception.

The other problem you may encounter with exceptions is in rethrowing the exception object. Exception objects are usually autoreleased. This means that, with manual memory management, they will be deleted when the current autorelease pool is deleted.

This is not a problem in most code. The autorelease pool you are most commonly using persists for the duration of the run loop. Sometimes, however, you will create your own autorelease pool.

If you drained your autorelease pool in an **@finally** block, as appears to be the obvious solution, you would encounter a problem. The exception object would be deleted while unwinding through your stack frame, and the next stack frame up would probably crash, dereferencing an orphaned pointer while looking up the type of the exception.

To avoid this, you need to make sure you retain the exception object before you delete the autorelease pool and then autorelease it

Note: In Java, you can use exceptions as a local goto as well, advertising a code path to the VM as being unusual, by throwing an exception and catching it in the same method. This is also possible in Objective-C, but it's incredibly inefficient. The @throw() statement will call the objc_exception_throw() function, which will call an unwind library function.

This will then read the DWARF data for the stack frame and call the Objective-C personality function. This function will then read more of the DWARF data, compare the class of the exception against the class of the catch block, and then set the instruction pointer to the address of the catch statement.

In Java, the VM will just translate this into an unconditional jump to the catch block. If you must use this pattern, then use a C **goto** statement in Objective-C. It's generally better to avoid it altogether, however, and find a solution that doesn't ignore the ideas of structured programming.

again afterward. This is one of the reasons why it's a bad idea to throw anything other than an **NSException** object. Anyone who follows the suggestion in Apple's documentation for doing this will end up with code that only correctly handles **NSException** objects and will prematurely destroy any other object type.

To implement this correctly, you need a catch-all
clause: an **@catch** clause with a **id** type. This
will catch all Objective-C exceptions. Remember
that C++ exceptions will still not be caught in
this block, so you still need an **@finally** block
to handle cleanup if you are unwinding with a
foreign exception. You can set the pointer to the
autorelease pool to **nil** in the **@catch** clause to
prevent it from being released twice.

Passing Error Delegates

```
23   NSFileManager *fm = [NSFileManager defaultManager
          ];
24   [fm copyPath: source
25        toPath: destination
26        handler: [ErrorHandler new]];
```

From: errordelegate.m

In Common Lisp, you have the idea of *resumable
exceptions*. These are contrasted with unwinding
exceptions like those found in Objective-C, Java,
C++, and so on. A resumable exception does
not unwind the stack; it runs the exception-
handling code and then continues.

In Objective-C there is no direct analogue, but
you can achieve the result by passing an *error
delegate* as an argument to a method. The
older APIs in **NSFileHandle** work this way.
The last argument to them is an object that is
sent messages when the operation encounters a

problem.

This method returns a **BOOL** indicating whether the operation should proceed. You can combine this with unwinding exceptions in your code by throwing an exception if the error delegate did not handle the conditions.

I used this pattern in the LanguageKit framework for reporting compiler errors and warnings. When the compiler encounters an error, it calls a method in the error delegate. The default implementation of this just dumped the message to the console, but other implementations transform the abstract syntax tree to remove the error. If this returns **YES**, the compiler backtracks and tries the check again. If it returns **NO** the compiler throws an exception, which is caught by the code that invoked the compiler.

In general, you should use this pattern anywhere you might encounter a fixable problem in the middle of an operation. For example, you could use it while loading a file that references other files. If one of the referenced files is missing the default option would be to abort. However, an error delegate could provide a new path, either by using some fixed translation or by prompting the user.

Returning Error Values

```
4    - (BOOL)trySomething;
5    - (id)tryToDoSomethingWithObject: (id)anObject
6                            error: (NSError**)e;
```

From: errorReturn.m

In C, a common pattern is to return zero on
success and some nonzero value to indicate an
error condition. This is much less popular in
Objective-C, but it is relatively common to
return a **BOOL** value representing whether an
operation succeeded.

Most of the time, this is done with methods that
mutate the receiver in some way. When you call
this kind of method, it is to affect some kind of
change in the object, not to get a value, so the
return value is not being used for anything else.

An example of this pattern is the
-setProperty:forKey: method on **NSStream**.
This tries to set a property of the stream and
returns **YES** if it succeeded. Note that this is the
opposite of the C pattern, which returns true on
failure.

Using NSError

```
6    NSError *error = nil;
7    NSStringEncoding enc;
8    NSString *str = [NSString
9       stringWithContentsOfFile: @"DoesNotExist"
10                 usedEncoding: &enc
11                        error: &error];
12   if (nil != error)
13   {
14     NSLog(@"Error: %@",
15        [error localizedDescription]);
16   }
```

From: nserror.m

A few of the methods that Apple introduced
with OS X 10.2 take an **NSString**** as an
argument. This is used to return a second value
reporting an error. If the variable that this
points to is **nil** after the call, the operation
succeeded. If not, it contains a string describing
error.

This had some obvious limitations. A string
is fine for reporting to the user, but it's not
particularly useful for recovering from the error.
If you want to handle the error in code, you need
to parse the string somehow.

When Apple released Safari, with 10.2.7, they
added a new class: **NSError**. This is almost
always returned via a pointer passed as the
last argument to a method. The error object
looks quite similar to the exception object. It
has a name (called a *domain*) and a dictionary

associated with it.

Unlike the exception object, the dictionary has several predefined keys. These include the localized error description. You can present this to the user without any extra processing.

Error objects also sometimes include a recovery strategy. The *recovery attempter* object can try to automatically recover from an error. For some errors this is not possible, but often you get an error when you try to do something that is possible, but unsafe. When this happens, you should present the error to the user and then call the recovery attempter.

If you have used Common Lisp, this pattern will seem familiar as an ad-hoc form of restartable exception.

13

Accessing Directories and Files

If you're using AppKit, you have two options for most filesystem-related tasks. The `NSFileManager` class, from the Foundation framework, provides a lot of low-level methods for manipulating files and directories. The `NSWorkspace` class from the Application Kit provides more abstract forms.

A number of the functions of `NSWorkspace` are delegated to the *workspace process*. On old NeXT systems, this was a single program, whereas on OS X, various bits of its functionality are implemented by the window server and the Finder.

Because of this, it doesn't make sense to think about using the higher-level versions when

the workspace process is not guaranteed to be
present—for example, in command-line tools
that might be run over a remote connection or
in server code.

The UIKit framework doesn't have an equivalent
of **NSWorkspace**. If you are targeting Cocoa
Touch, you have to use the lower-level APIs.

Reading a File

```
7    NSData *copy =
8      [NSData dataWithContentsOfFile: file];
9    NSData *mapped =
10     [NSData dataWithContentsOfMappedFile: file];
11   NSData *read = [[NSFileHandle
12       fileHandleForReadingAtPath: file]
13       readDataToEndOfFile];
```

From: readFile.m

UNIX systems typically offer two ways of
accessing a file: The **read()** and **mmap()** system
calls. Most other systems—at least those that
run on hardware with a *memory management
unit (MMU)*—have equivalents of these. The
first copies a stream of bytes from a file into a
buffer. The second maps the file's data into a
region of memory.

Foundation provides two classes that correspond
roughly to these operations. The **NSData** class
encapsulates a region of memory containing
untyped data. You can create instances of this
class from files with a variety of options.

For small files, you can just use the version that
wraps the **read()** call and reads a copy of the
file's data into memory. For larger files, you may
wish to use **+dataWithContentsOfMappedFile:**.

The advantage of the latter approach is that it
interacts very well with the operating system's
virtual memory subsystem. If you run out of
physical memory, you don't need to allocate
swap space for evicting pages that contain data
from a mapped file; you can just discard them
and read them back in the next time they are
accessed.

This is very useful if you are on a platform with
very little memory and no virtual memory. The
iPhones before the 3GS, for example, only have
128MB of RAM, and none of them have any
swap space. If you read a 4MB file into memory,
you have used up a large chunk of the space
available to your application.

If, in contrast, you create a mapped data object
representing the file, the system will read in
the data in 4KB chunks, as it's needed, and
evict it when it is no longer required. If you run
out of memory when creating a new object, for
example, the kernel will evict the mapped file
from memory to make space. It can't do this if
you had read the file, so it would just run out of
memory and kill your application.

If you only want to read a bit of a file at a time,
you should use **NSFileHandle**. This class wraps
a file descriptor and implements Objective-C

versions of the same basic operations that the
C standard library supports. You can read all of
the data from a file handle in a single operation,
but more often you will read the next available
bit.

You can read a fixed-size chunk of data by
sending the file handle a **-readDataOfLength:**
message. Most of the other methods on this class
are not particularly interesting for reading data
from a file; they are intended for interacting with
sockets. We'll look at this class again in Chapter
17.

Moving and Copying Files

```
12   NSFileManager *fm = [NSFileManager new];
13   if (shouldMove)
14   {
15     [fm copyItemAtPath: source
16               toPath: destination
17                error: nil];
18   }
19   else
20   {
21     [fm moveItemAtPath: source
22               toPath: destination
23                error: nil];
24   }
```

From: fileCopy.m

The **NSFileManager** class encapsulates the
filesystem as a whole and lets you manipulate
it. This class exposes to Objective-C developers
the same kind of features that Apple's Finder

and the Windows Explorer expose to the user.

Prior to OS X 10.5, the methods you used took an object as the last parameter. This object was then sent messages while the copy or move operation proceeded. These messages, for example, asked whether to proceed after an error.

With 10.5, Apple decided to change the interface considerably. The methods now use the new error-reporting pattern that we discussed in Chapter 12, so the last argument is a pointer to an **NSError*** used to return an error. The messages are now sent to the object's delegate.

This means that you must now only use an **NSFileManager** from a single thread. Prior to 10.5, this class was an example of the *singleton pattern.* It was very common to cache the return value from the **+defaultManager** method, which returned the singleton instance. Now, this is unsafe if code that uses the cached version might be called from different threads.

If you are writing new code, you should make sure you create a new **NSFileManager** instance every time you want to use it and destroy it afterward, otherwise you may end up with messages being sent to the wrong delegate. If you don't, two threads can concurrently set the delegate for the singleton file manager and one receive all of the notifications, rather than each receive the notifications it's interested in.

If you use the old, deprecated methods on the

Note: This is an example of thoughtless
software design. A better solution would have
been to store the delegate in the *thread dictionary*
(see Chapter 14). If you are ever in the position
of making similar changes to a singleton class,
consider this approach, or simply retain the extra
parameter for a callback. Don't require invasive
changes to existing code to support your new
interfaces.

---

file manager, it is thread safe with the singleton.
If you are not calling any methods that send
delegate messages, it is also safe to use the
singleton. This is unfortunate, because it means
you may need to create a new **NSFileManager**
instance when you copy a file, even if you
already have a pointer to the singleton instance.

Getting File Attributes

```
6    NSFileManager *fm = [NSFileManager defaultManager
         ];
7    NSDictionary *attrs =
8      [fm attributesOfItemAtPath: @"fileAttributes.m"
9                         error: NULL];
10   NSString *fileType = [attrs fileType];
11   NSNumber *creator =
12     [attrs objectForKey: NSFileHFSCreatorCode];
```

From: fileAttributes.m

The **NSFileManager** class wraps most of the

standard POSIX filesystem manipulation functions. In C, you would typically use the `stat()` function to find information about a file. This function takes a pointer to a structure as an argument and fills it in with information about the file.

The limitation of this is obvious: You can't add new fields to the structure without breaking all existing code that uses it. The `NSFileManager` version is much more flexible. The `-attributesOfItemAtPath:error:` method returns an `NSDictionary`, and it is trivial to add extra entries to a dictionary without breaking binary compatibility.

One thing you will note from this example is that we can send a `-fileType` message to the dictionary to get the value. This method is part of `NSDictionary` and returns the dictionary entry that corresponds to the `NSFileType` key. There are a few other, similar dictionary methods.

On OS X, you have a few more bits of file metadata than on other POSIX platforms. HFS+ stores a creator code and a type code for each file. These are not used as much now, but on Classic MacOS they were used instead of file extensions to determine the correct application to open a file.

Manipulating Paths

```
 6    NSString *home = @"~";
 7    NSString *full =
 8      [home stringByExpandingTildeInPath];
 9    NSString *users =
10      [full stringByDeletingLastPathComponent];
11    NSString *file =
12      [users stringByAppendingPathComponent: @"users"
             ];
13    NSString *fileWithExtension =
14      [file stringByAppendingPathExtension: @"db"];
```

From: path.m

A lot of UNIX code manipulates paths by using the sscanf() and sprintf() functions. This then causes a lot of problems when you come to port the code to Windows or Symbian, for example, where the filesystem layout and path separator are different.

OpenStep was designed from the start to be portable across different operating system families. The NSString class provides a few methods designed for manipulating paths.

Although these manipulate strings, they expose an interface that is more abstract. You can add or remove path components, which are single entries in a path (either files or directories). You can also modify the file extension.

On OS X, like any UNIX system, there is a single root folder, represented by a single slash. Subdirectories are separated by a slash, and file extensions are separated by a dot. On Windows, there are multiple roots, path components are separated by a backslash, but file extensions are still separated by a dot.

If you use the path manipulation methods on `NSString`, your code will work correctly irrespective of the filesystem conventions.

Unfortunately, `NSMutableString` does not have a corresponding set of operations. You can avoid some of the overhead of creating lots of temporary objects by using the `+pathWithComponents:` and `-pathComponents` methods, which construct a string from an array of path components, and create an array of path components, respectively.

It's not worth worrying too much about efficiency in code that deals with paths. Pretty much any operation on the filesystem will be a lot more expensive than creating a few temporary objects.

Determining if a File or Directory Exists

```
9    NSFileManager *fm =
10     [NSFileManager defaultManager];
11   BOOL isDir;
12   if ([fm fileExistsAtPath: path
13               isDirectory: &isDir])
14   {
15     if (isDir)
16       printf("Folder exists\n");
17     else
18       printf("File exists\n");
19   }
20   else
21     printf("File does not exist\n");
```

From: fileExists.m

The simplest way of determining whether a file exists is to try to access it and then check for errors. This isn't particularly elegant, although it is often the safe way to work. If you want to provide some feedback to the user about whether an operation is expected to work, before trying it, you need an explicit test.

The -fileExistsAtPath:isDirectory: method does exactly this. The method's name is a bit misleading. It tests whether a file or directory exists at the specified path, and tells you if it is a directory.

The second parameter is a pointer to a **BOOL**. If you're coming from C or C++, this will seem quite familiar, but for people coming from

Note: Don't use this mechanism to create temporary files. If you do, there is a potential race condition between testing whether the file exists and creating it. Use the C library `mkstemp()` function instead. The EtoileFoundation framework has a wrapper around this that you can use if you want to stay in object land.

languages like Java it may seem a bit unusual.

C, and by extension Objective-C, only supports returning a single value, but this method needs to return two things: whether something exists and whether it is a directory. There are a few ways of implementing this. One would be to define an enumerated type, with nothing exists, file exists, and directory exists elements.

This would have made all of the code that uses this method simpler, so it's not immediately obvious why it wasn't done. The answer becomes apparent when you realize that you can pass NULL as the second argument. If you do this, the method will not bother testing whether the object at that path is a directory. This is a relatively small saving, so it's not clear that this was a sensible design choice.

Working with Bundles

```
6    NSBundle *mainBundle =
7      [NSBundle mainBundle];
8    NSLog(@"%@ links against: %@",
9      [mainBundle executablePath],
10     [NSBundle allFrameworks]);
```

From: bundles.m

On Apple System 7 and earlier, the filesystem supported two forks: a code fork and a data fork. The data fork was used to store arbitrary resources. With Mac OS 8.1, Apple introduced HFS+, which supported an arbitrary number of forks, making files effectively the same as directories in their ability to contain arbitrary numbers of children. NTFS has the same functionality.

OS X still supports resource forks and will store the data in a hidden file on filesystems that do not support them, such as UFS and FAT, but their use is not recommended. Copying files that contain forks to other filesystems is a problem. If you copy a file to a FAT disk with OS X and then copy it from that disk with Windows, you will not copy the hidden file, so the data in the fork will be lost.

Meanwhile, NeXT went in a different direction. If forks make files like directories, why not just use directories instead? NeXTSTEP provided functionality like forks on top of a standard UNIX filesystem, just by using directories in place of files.

Directories that are supposed to be treated as files are called *bundles*. To primitive low-level filesystem operations, and to other operating systems, they look like directories. If you copy an OS X application bundle, for example, to a USB drive and then look at it on Windows, it will just look like any other directory. When you look at it in the Finder, however, it will look like a single file.

The two kinds of bundles you will use in almost any Objective-C program are frameworks and applications. These both contain some executable code (a program or a shared library) and a set of resources.

The exact layout depends on the system. GNUstep uses the older NeXT-style bundle layout, whereas OS X uses a slightly simpler one. You can quite easily produce bundles that have both the GNUstep and Cocoa layouts, allowing the same .app bundle to be portable between systems without recompiling.

You can get the main bundle for an application by sending a +mainBundle message to NSBundle. This is a class that is used to encapsulate bundles. It keeps track of all dynamically loaded bundles.

Bundles are naturally localizable. Resources are stored in different subdirectories for each locale and can be loaded on demand. The -pathForResource:ofType: method will return

Note: Command-line tools are typically not stored in bundles. They still have a main bundle object, however. This object has the directory containing the main executable as its path.

the localized version of a named resource, with the specified extension, in the bundle's resources directory.

You can use this in your code to get the localized version of a resource file stored in your application bundle or from any loaded bundles. If your code is in a framework, you might want to get resources from the framework bundle. This is slightly more complicated than getting code from the main bundle.

The `+bundleForClass:` method will give you the bundle that contains the code for a specified class. If you think you might move a class into a framework in the future, it's a good idea to use this method when loading resources.

Finding Files in System Locations

```
11    NSArray *dirs =
12      NSSearchPathForDirectoriesInDomains(
13        NSLibraryDirectory,
14        NSAllDomainsMask,
15        YES);
```

From: frameworkLoader.m

On OS X, the filesystem layout is quite well defined. You can probably hard-code paths and expect things to work. If you port your code to other platforms, you will find that things break quite significantly.

This was one of the problems that OpenStep programmers encountered quite often. Porting code between Solaris, OPENSTEP, and Windows NT, for example, required changing a lot of hard-coded paths for each platform.

After Apple bought NeXT, they released a new version of OPENSTEP with a MacOS compatibility layer and a new user interface called Rhapsody. This used the same NeXT filesystem hierarchy as OPENSTEP, complete with a /NeXT folder in the root containing the non-UNIX-like parts of the hierarchy.

With Rhapsody DR2, Apple made some significant changes to the directory layout and introduced the layout that is now familiar to OS X users. To make life easier, and to support YellowBox (Cocoa) for Windows, a product that

was discontinued soon after, they introduced
the `NSSearchPathForDirectoriesInDomains()`
function.

This function returns an array of directories for
a specific use. When you call this function, the
first argument describes the kind of directory
you want. This might be an applications
directory, a library directory, and so on. The
second is the *filesystem domain*.

OS X, like OPENSTEP, divides the filesystem
hierarchy into a number of domains that all have
roughly the same contents, but for different uses.
These are ordered, so you should prefer files in
higher-priority domains. The four domains are as
follows:

User This domain is inside the user's home
directory. Files here are private to the user
and completely under the user's control.

Local The domain containing files local to the
machine. On OS X, this includes things
such as the /**Library** directory that may be
modified by the local system administrator.

Network It is quite rare to see anything in this
domain. You will not see it on stand-alone
machines, or on machines that are part
of a heterogeneous network. It is used
for directories controlled by the network
administrator.

System The final domain contains system files.
In general, you should never write to any

location in this domain, although you can
read from it. Any modifications that you
make may be reverted the next time the
user updates the system.

Not every type of directory exists in every
domain. For example, there is no documents
directory in the system domain, and it would
not make sense if there were.

The final argument tells the function whether
to expand tildes in the paths. You will almost
always pass **YES** here.

The frameworkLoader.m example shows several
of the things we've looked at in this chapter.
This example loads a named framework. Because
frameworks are bundles, you can use **NSBundle**
for loading them.

This example first gets a list of all of the
Library directories in the system. It then looks
in them in order to test whether a directory
exists in each of them that has the name of the
framework and the .framework extension.

If something with the right name exists, the
example program tells **NSBundle** to load it. You
can use this code to lazily load frameworks at
run time, rather than linking to them explicitly.
Alternatively, you can modify it to look in a
plugins directory for your application in the
library directory, in which case you should look
in **NSApplicationSupportDirectory**. If you
build plugins as bundles, you will load them in
exactly the same way.

```objc
NSArray *dirs =
  NSSearchPathForDirectoriesInDomains(
    NSLibraryDirectory,
    NSAllDomainsMask,
    YES);
for (NSString *dir in dirs)
{
  NSString *f =
    [[[dir stringByAppendingPathComponent: @"
        Frameworks"]
      stringByAppendingPathComponent: framework]
       stringByAppendingPathExtension: @"
          framework"];
  // Check that the framework exists and is a
      directory.
  BOOL isDir = NO;
  if ([fm fileExistsAtPath: f
                isDirectory: &isDir]
    && isDir)
  {
    NSBundle *bundle =
      [NSBundle bundleWithPath: f];
    if ([bundle load])
    {
      NSLog(@"Loaded bundle %@", f);
      return YES;
    }
  }
}
```

From: frameworkLoader.m

14

Threads

The original NeXT operating system was built on top of Mach, just as OS X is. Mach supported threads from the very start and was one of the first UNIX-like systems to do so. More recently, the POSIX threading APIs have provided a cross-platform way of creating and manipulating threads.

On OS X, POSIX threads are implemented on top of Mach threads and Objective-C threads are implemented on top of POSIX threads. You will almost certainly not want to use Mach threads directly—they do not quite match up to the UNIX process model and are tricky to use correctly—but you may wish to use some of the POSIX threading functions directly.

Creating Threads

```objc
10  - (void)processInNewThread
11  {
12    SEL sel = @selector(process:);
13    [NSThread
14      detachNewThreadSelector: sel
15                     toTarget: self
16                   withObject: nil];
17  }
```

From: thread.m

Threads in Objective-C are encapsulated in **NSThread** objects. These wrap a POSIX thread and provide some convenience methods.

As of 10.5, there are two ways of creating new threads. The traditional one is similar to the standard way of creating POSIX threads, whereas the second is intended to be more familiar to Java programmers.

When you create a new POSIX thread, you call a function with a **void**∗ parameter in a new thread. When you create a new thread using **NSThread**, you do something similar, sending a message to an object, taking another object as an argument.

The more Java-like way of creating a new thread is to subclass **NSThread** and override the −**main** method. You can then create a new instance of your thread object and send it a −**start** message to start it running.

When you create a new thread, it does not

have an autorelease pool in place, so the most common thing to do first is either create an autorelease pool, or create a new run loop for the thread.

Creating a new thread is a relatively expensive operation in Objective-C, just as it is in C. The process must get some new memory for the new thread's stack from the kernel, create all of the userspace and kernel data structures for scheduling it, and map some additional space for thread-local storage. It's therefore a good idea to keep threads around for a while once you've created them.

Creating a new run loop in the thread is a good way of doing this. You can then register timers to fire, monitor file descriptors for new data, and use an event-driven style of programming in the new thread.

Controlling Thread Priority

```
6   double oldPriority =
7     [NSThread threadPriority];
8   [NSThread setThreadPriority: 0];
9   [[NSThread mainThread]
10    setThreadPriority: 1];
```

From: threadPriority.m

The NSThread implements **threadPriority** and **setThreadPriority** methods as both class and instance methods. When sent to the class, they control the priority of the current thread. When sent to an instance, they control the priority of the thread encapsulated by that object.

The priority of a thread determines how much CPU time it will get and how long it has to wait between being given access to the CPU. With the lower-level POSIX APIs for controlling thread priority, you can also set the scheduler policy. The functions for doing this are all part of the POSIX realtime extensions, which also provide signal queues and so on. This is not exposed (yet) by the Objective-C APIs.

Priorities set with this API are double-precision floating-point values between 0 and 1. These will be scaled to some integer range that the scheduler understands, so you should remember that small differences will be rounded.

The POSIX specification defines two *contention scopes* for threads. A thread's priority defines a base value for whether it should be allowed CPU time, which is scaled based how much it has already had and how long since it last had any. The contention scope determines which threads compete for CPU time. With a system contention scope, the thread competes with all other threads in the system. With a process contention scope, it only competes with threads owned by the same process.

OS X only implements the system scope, which means that a high-priority thread will steal processor time away from threads in other processes at a lower priority. If you set a thread priority greater than 0.5, remember that this can have an adverse affect on the rest of the system.

This still won't cause complete starvation. With OS X 10.6, the highest thread priority gives a little bit more than double the amount of CPU time that the lowest priority is awarded, in purely CPU-bound tasks. Most tasks will involve some time waiting for data from the disk. Threads in a blocking state do not consume any CPU time irrespective of their priority.

The scheduling policy on OS X contradicts the traditional UNIX model, where only the superuser can raise the priority of a process. Somewhat interestingly, the thread priority on recent versions of OS X actually has a greater impact on the amount of CPU time a thread gets than the priority of the process that owns it. This means that, although you cannot raise the process's priority, you can achieve the same effect by raising the priority of all of the threads in your process.

The original design to prevent normal users from increasing process priority was to prevent one user from getting an unfair amount of CPU time. OS X systems tend to be single-user machines, so this is less of an issue, but you can still take processor time away from more important tasks owned by the same user. A live video capture, for example, is performance sensitive and the user would probably be very irritated if your program decided to set its priority high enough to cause the capturing application to drop frames.

Be considerate when setting thread priorities. In general, you should only use the range between 0 and 0.5. Only set a thread above the default level if you have absolutely no other option. Don't do it just because you are doing something CPU-bound and you want it to be fast.

Synchronizing Threads

```
3   static NSLock *lock;
4   static NSMutableArray *messages;
5
6   void recordLogMessage(NSString *msg)
7   {
8     [lock lock];
9     @try
10    {
11      [messages addObject: msg];
12      NSLog(@"%@", msg);
13    }
14    @finally
15    {
16      [lock unlock];
17    }
18  }
```

From: lock.m

You can synchronize two threads in several ways. The classes that perform this kind of synchronization all conform to the **NSLocking** protocol. This defines two methods: **-lock** and

-unlock.

The simplest lock class is NSLock, which implements a *mutual exclusion lock (mutex)*. One thread can lock this at a time, so sending it a -lock message will cause any other thread that sends the same object a -lock message to block until you send a corresponding -unlock message.

This is useful for protecting critical sections that are short. For longer critical sections, NSRecursiveLock is often more useful. If you send two -lock messages to an NSLock in the same thread, you have a deadlock. You can send as many -lock messages as you want to an NSRecursiveLock as long as you send the same number of -unlock messages. This is useful in methods that may be called from code that has already acquired the lock, as well as from code that hasn't.

The problem with these classes, traditionally, is that they didn't integrate well with exception handling. If you acquired a lock and then called something that threw an exception, you would have problems. The lock would never be released.

When Apple introduced the new exception-handling keywords, they also introduced **@synchronized**. This will lock on an arbitrary object and make sure that the lock is released if an exception is thrown.

Generally speaking, it is a bad idea to use

this keyword. Although it makes life a little easier, and is familiar to Java programmers, the implementation is very inefficient. It needs to associate a lock with the object, and it always uses a recursive lock even when this isn't ideal. You can achieve the same effect by making sure that you send the **-unlock** message in an **@finally** block.

You can avoid the **@try** and **@finally** block if you are sure that none of the called methods or functions will throw an exception, but with the GNU and Modern Apple runtimes they don't have any run-time penalty.

Storing Thread-Specific Data

```
6   NSMutableDictionary *threadDict =
7     [[NSThread currentThread] threadDictionary];
8   [threadDict setObject: @"default"
9                  forKey: @"NewKey"];
```

From: threadDict.m

Once you have threads, you often want to store some data privately to the thread. An example of this in Cocoa is the current graphics context, which must be available to any code that is drawing, but must not be shared between threads.

Typically, you implement this using the **pthread_set_specific()** function, which stores a pointer associated with the current thread. This is commonly implemented by storing the address of a region of memory in a register and using a fixed offset from the start of that region for each bit of thread-specific data. That means you need to have space for every thread-local pointer in every thread, even if you only set one of them to something other than NULL.

If Cocoa stored the graphics context like this, every single thread would require one word of space, even though most programs only need a valid graphics context in one, or possibly two, threads.

The solution to this is the **thread dictionary**. This is a mutable dictionary associated with the thread. You only need one word per thread to store this pointer, but you can store as many objects in it as you want. Only threads that have a value associated with a given key need to have space to store it.

The thread dictionary is accessed by sending a `-threadDictionary` message to the current thread. You can then manipulate it like any other dictionary. When the thread exits, the dictionary is destroyed. Because dictionaries retain their arguments, this means that any objects only referenced from the thread dictionary will be freed, after their destructors run.

You can use this to run code when a thread exits, but it's not recommended. Threads will post an `NSThreadWillExitNotification` before they exit, so you can just observe this if you want to run some cleanup code.

Note: On most platforms, you can use the
__thread keyword, a GCC extension that stores
variables in thread-local storage. The Darwin
loader does not support thread-local sections, so
this is not possible on OS X. This will probably
change soon, as similar functionality is in the next
versions of both the C and C++ standards.

The thread dictionary provides a good way
of passing parameters between nested stack
frames. Sometimes you want to set some semi-
global state that will persist for the duration of
a method call and be accessible from all methods
inside that scope.

The classical Cocoa example is the graphics
context object, which is set at the root of the
view hierarchy and then modified and used
by all nested calls. In LanguageKit, I use the
same pattern to allow AST nodes to access
the compiler object. In both cases, the lack of
tight coupling means that the same method—on
the same object—can be called in two different
threads, with different contexts.

Waiting for a Condition

```
19   - (void)addToQueue
20   {
21     [condition lock];
22     queueSize++;
23     [condition signal];
24     [condition unlock];
25   }
26   - (void)main
27   {
28     while (1)
29     {
30       id pool = [NSAutoreleasePool new];
31       [condition lock];
32       while (queueSize == 0)
33       {
34         [condition wait];
35       }
36       queueSize--;
37       [condition unlock];
38       NSLog(@"Processed data from queue");
39       [pool release];
40     }
41   }
```

From: condition.m

Quite often, you want to have one thread
sleep and wake up when another thread does
something. The POSIX thread API provides
condition variables for this.

A condition variable is paired with a mutex.
When you wait on a condition variable, you
first acquire the mutex, then atomically release
it and sleep on the condition variable. When
the condition variable is signalled, you wake and
atomically reacquire the mutex. You can think of

condition variables as a way of passing a mutex between threads.

The OpenStep specification included a class encapsulating this low-level primitive: `NSConditionLock`. Unlike the POSIX version, which needs to be associated with a mutex on each call, this class contains its own mutex and implements the `NSLocking` protocol.

This means that you can use a condition lock as a lock, although that would be wasteful. As well as the lock, the condition lock also has an integer variable associated with it, representing the condition. When you sleep on a condition lock, you can specify a value. Your thread will then not be awoken until the condition lock is signalled with this value.

The condition lock is quite convenient when the condition you are waiting for is an integer value, but less so in other cases. Often, you want a thread to wake up when an object enters a particular state. This is quite easy with the low-level POSIX functions, because they expect you to test the condition yourself, but is less easy with the `NSConditionLock`.

To address this, Apple introduced the `NSCondition` class. This is a simple wrapper around a POSIX mutex and condition variable. You can lock it, sleep on it releasing the lock, and then signal it from another thread to wake it up.

When you wake after sleeping on an

`NSCondition`, the condition object will be locked. You must test your condition and then either unlock the condition object or go back to sleep.

You use the same pattern with condition variables in almost every case you will use them. Generally, they let you establish a producer-consumer relationship between threads. The consumer thread needs to sleep until there is some data waiting for it. The producer threads need to wake up the consumer thread when there is some data for it.

The example at the start of this section showed two methods on a class. The `-addToQueue` method is expected to be called from a producer thread, whereas the `-main` method implements the consumer thread.

The consumer thread code shows several important features of a threaded object. Rather than using an `NSRunLoop`, this implements its own run loop, an infinite loop, and creates and destroys an autorelease pool at every iteration explicitly. In each iteration, it first locks the condition and then, if there is no data waiting, releases the lock and sleeps.

A producer thread can then acquire the lock and signal the condition. When this happens, the consumer thread will be poised to wake up as soon as the lock becomes available. The producer permits this by releasing the lock.

The consumer thread then gets the next bit of

data to process and releases the lock. In this example, incrementing and decrementing a shared variable is used as a proxy for adding some data to a shared data structure.

Note: The sequence of operations required to wake a thread from a condition variable is quite expensive, so it's worth avoiding if possible. For communicating between two threads, I generally prefer to use a lockless ring buffer that switches to a locked mode after it has been empty for a while. Apple's Grand Central Dispatch implements this model internally, so you can use it without having to write the ring buffer code yourself.

15

Blocks and Grand Central

One of the most recent additions to Objective-C is support for *blocks*, also known as *closures*. Blocks were part of Smalltalk, but omitted in Objective-C for several reasons. Smalltalk used them for flow control, while Objective-C inherits C flow control primitives, so does not require them. The extra complexity in the compiler and runtime library, along with the speed penalty, meant that they were not a high priority for Objective-C, initially.

A closure is a function that can be created inside some other scope and can refer to variables inside that scope. Normally, a function may refer to three things: globals, arguments, and local variables. It may only exist in the global scope. In contrast, a block may be declared inside a function, or even inside another block. It may refer to any variables that are visible where the block is declared.

Binding Variables to Blocks

```
3   int (^add)(int, int) =
4     ^(int a, int b)
5     {
6       return a + b;
7     };
```

From: blockScope.m

You can think of functions as a special case
of blocks. A function, conceptually, is a block
that is declared in the global scope. They are
implemented in a slightly different way, but the
differences are very small in this case.

The simplest case for a block, therefore,
is equivalent to a function. It takes some
arguments, produces some output, and doesn't
refer to anything outside of its own scope. The
snippet at the start of this section shows an
example of this kind of block. This declaration is
at the global scope, and looks like a very verbose
form of a function declaration.

The next kind of block refers to things in the
scope of the function where it was declared.
You can see a block of this kind in the rest of
blockScope.m.

This block refers to two variables. **counter** is a
static variable, which means that it is stored in
some memory mapped from the program image,

> **Note:** Although there is only one type of block exposed to the programmer, there are two in the implementation. You can find out which kind of block you have by inspecting the isa pointer, although this is not guaranteed by the public API and is subject to change without notice.
>
> If you create a block that does not refer to anything other than its parameters or global variables, then the block is statically allocated, and every time it is conceptually created, you will get a pointer to the same object.
>
> If you create a block that refers to things on the stack, then the blocks runtime will create a new copy of it on the heap every time that it is created.

just like a global. The reference to this in the block will work just like a reference to any other static or global; only one copy of the variable exists.

The other variable, c, is a local variable. This is allocated on the stack in the **getCounter()** function. When that function returns, the variable is destroyed. The block still exists, but it refers to a copy of the variable. This means that c inside the block always contains the value that c had when the block was created. You can see in the output how this works. Each block prints the value of the counter when it was created and the current value.

```
10   void(^getCounter(void))(void)
11   {
12     static int counter;
13     int c = counter;
14     void(^block)(void) = ^(void)
15     {
16       printf("current: %d ", counter);
17       printf("old: %d\n", c);
18     };
19     counter++;
20     return Block_copy(block);
21   }
22
23   int main(void)
24   {
25     void(^block)(void) = getCounter();
26     block(); block();
27     void(^block2)(void) = getCounter();
28     block2(); block2();
29     block(); block();
30     return 0;
31   }
```

From: blockScope.m

```
1   current: 1 old: 0
2   current: 1 old: 0
3   current: 2 old: 1
4   current: 2 old: 1
5   current: 2 old: 0
6   current: 2 old: 0
```

Output from: blockScope

A traditional closure refers to the real variables
in the enclosing scope, not copies. You can get

this behavior by declaring the variable with
the __block qualifier. The implementation of
this is very complicated. The variable is moved
from the stack into a reference counted bit of
code in heap memory. This means that every
reference to it will refer to the same variable.
The blockCapture.m example demonstrates
this, with a function that creates two, linked,
counters.

```
3    typedef int(^counter_t)(void);
4
5    void linkedCounters(counter_t *a, counter_t *b)
6    {
7      __block int c = 0;
8      *a = ^(void) { return c++; };
9      *b = ^(void) { return ++c; };
10     *a = Block_copy(*a);
11     *b = Block_copy(*b);
12     c++;
13   }
14
15   int main(void)
16   {
17     counter_t pre, post;
18     linkedCounters(&post, &pre);
19     printf("%d %d, %d, %d\n",
20       pre(), post(), pre(), post());
21     return 0;
22   }
```

From: blockCapture.m

Both of these counters refer to the same variable
in memory: one returns it then increments it;
the other increments it then returns it. When

you run this program, you will see that calling one block affects the return value the next time that you call the other.

```
1    2 2, 4, 4
```

Output from: blockCapture

The next time that you call the `linkedCounters()` function, you will get a new pair of blocks, referring to a new counter variable. Note the difference between the **static** and __block storage qualifiers. Both have a similar effect, moving a variable off the stack, and allowing it to persist longer than the function, but they work very differently.

When you declare a variable as **static**, every single reference to it will refer to the same piece of memory. When you declare a variable as __block, every reference to it from the same scope will refer to the same bit of memory, but you will get a new copy every time that you enter the scope in which it is declared.

Managing Memory with Blocks

```
5   __block int counter;
6   int(^block)(void) =
7     ^(void) { return counter++; };
8   block = [block copy];
9   Block_release(block);
```

From: blockMemory.m

Memory management in Cocoa traditionally uses reference counting. Blocks work in the same way. There are two functions controlling the reference count of a block. The **_Block_copy()** function increases its reference count, while the **_Block_release()** function decreases it.

The first function is not called **_Block_retain()**, to make it explicit that the returned block may not be the block passed as an argument. In some situations, the block might be allocated on the stack, then copied onto the heap when it is copied. Most of the time, you won't call these functions directly. Instead, you will use macros that lack the leading underscore prefix. These macros wrap the functions and ensure that the return type is the same as the argument type.

In Objective-C, you can also send blocks –retain, –release, and –autorelease messages, just as you can any other object. In fact, you can send blocks any messages that you want, but they only respond to a few. The compiler won't give a warning if you send any messages to blocks, but you will get a run-time exception.

You should be very careful about sending -retain messages to blocks. The contract for this method requires that it return the receiver. You must use -copy to ensure that stack blocks are copied to the heap. This is especially important in garbage collected mode, where -retain messages are silently ignored. In ARC mode, you don't need to call these functions or send these messages at all: ARC handles all memory management in blocks for you.

Memory management of variables referenced by blocks can be more difficult to understand. The blockRetain.m example shows two blocks that both refer to objects. The first gets a copy of the object pointer, the second gets a shared reference because of the __block storage qualifier.

```
5    id a = [@"a" mutableCopy];
6    __block id b = [@"b" mutableCopy];
7    unsigned long(^refCountA)() = ^()
8      { return [a retainCount]; };
9    unsigned long(^refCountB)() = ^()
10     { return [b retainCount]; };
11   printf("%ld %ld\n", refCountA(), refCountB());
12   refCountA = Block_copy(refCountA);
13   refCountB = Block_copy(refCountB);
14   printf("%ld %ld\n", refCountA(), refCountB());
15   [refCountA release]; [refCountB release];
16   printf("%ld %ld\n", [a retainCount], [b
         retainCount]);
```

From: blockRetain.m

When you retain the block that has a copy of
the object pointer, the object is also implicitly
retained, automatically. Note that this only
happens once. When you retain the block
a second time, it is not. When the block is
destroyed, the object is released.

```
1   1 1
2   2 1
3   1 1152921504606846975
```

Output from: blockRetain

This is not the case for the second block. This
block has been freed, so sending it a message
has undefined behavior. In this particular run,
it returned some data from a random memory
location. It might alternatively crash.

It is your responsibility to ensure that the object
remains valid for as long as one or more of
the blocks persists. This is very difficult to do
correctly, because blocks, unlike objects, do not
have a way of registering cleanup code. This is
addressed if you compile in ARC mode. Blocks
will automatically retain any objects that are
stored in their bound variables and will release
them when the block itself is destroyed.

This is also a problem when a block refers to
other pointers. Even if a pointer does not have
the __block storage qualifier, the memory that
it references is not copied. This means that you
have to keep track of it just as you would any

other memory in C, with the added complication that the block, containing a reference to it, may persist for a long time.

Performing Actions in the Background

```
6    dispatch_queue_t q =
7        dispatch_get_global_queue(0,0);
8    __block int count;
9    dispatch_async(q, ^(void){ count++; });
10   sleep(1);
11   NSCAssert(count == 1,
12       @"Counter incremented in background");
```

From: libdispatch.m

If you are using Cocoa on OS X 10.6 or GNUstep on FreeBSD, then you have the option of using *libdispatch*, branded by Apple as Grand Central Dispatch, for concurrent processing. This library was written by Apple and released under the Apache 2 license. If you use libdispatch, you don't manage threads manually, you manage work queues.

Work queues execute work units of code and data. There are two sorts of queue, concurrent and FIFO. A concurrent queue will start executing work units in the order that they are added to the queue, but may execute more than one concurrently. A FIFO queue will wait for each unit to complete before starting the next one.

Queues do not have a 1:1 mapping with threads. Concurrent queues may execute on several threads and one thread may run work units from several queues. The optimal number of threads to use is determined by the kernel based on the number of cores and the system load.

Context switching between threads is relatively expensive. It obviously costs at least as much as setjmp(), because it needs to save the current CPU state and restore it later, but there are also some non-obvious costs. Different threads are likely to be accessing different bits of the program's data at the same time, so switching threads also causes a lot of cache and TLB misses.

With the work queue model, a single thread can run one work unit from one queue, then run one from another, without constantly switching between the two working sets. If you have more cores, you can increase the degree of concurrency to take advantage of them without increasing the number of context switches. When the system is busy, you may reduce the number of threads that one application is using so that it can use one core effectively while another application uses another. This is all done automatically by libdispatch.

Grand Central does not depend on blocks, but it is much easier to use in conjunction with blocks. In the simplest case, you just push blocks into a work queue and have them executed in the background. That's what the example at the start of this section does. It gets a handle to the default queue for the normal priority and pushes a block into it. The queue will then execute this in the background as soon as there is some spare CPU time.

Creating Custom Work Queues

```
5   dispatch_queue_t q =
6     dispatch_queue_create("Example",0);
7   __block int count;
8   dispatch_async(q, ^(void){ count++; });
9   dispatch_async(q, ^(void){ count++; });
10  dispatch_async(q, ^(void){ count++; });
11  dispatch_async(q, ^(void){ printf("%d\n", count)
       ;});
```

From: libdispatchFIFO.m

Grand Central comes with three concurrent queues, which are created by default. These are registered at three priority levels: low, default, and high. The number of things that will run concurrently on each of these depends on the load of the system and the number of CPU cores available. You can get a handle to one of these with the **dispatch_get_global_queue()** function that we saw in the last section.

There is no point in creating a new concurrent queue. Blocks pushed into a concurrent queue will begin executing in the order that they were pushed, but they may complete in an arbitrary order, and any number of them might be running at once.

There is also one special queue, which is intended to run on the main thread. You can get a reference to this with `dispatch_get_main_queue()`. This queue is used on OS X 10.6 to implement the run loop.

This queue is a FIFO queue, and you may wish to create similar queues. A FIFO queue is similar to a lightweight thread. It executes sequentially, one block at a time. The relationship between threads and queues is variable. All of your queues may end up running concurrently on separate threads, or all may be executed on a single OS thread, depending on various factors.

You create a new FIFO queue by calling `dispatch_queue_create()`. This is useful when you have a number of things that need to execute in a defined order, but are largely independent of the rest of the program. This helps reduce the need for explicit synchronization.

The example at the start of this chapter pushed three blocks that incremented a counter and one that printed its final value into a new queue. These blocks are all related; executing them in the wrong order is a very bad idea. With this approach, they all execute in a guaranteed order with respect to each other, but not with regard to the rest of the program. This means that you don't need to put any lock around the `counter` variable, unless you plan on accessing it from outside of the queue.

16

Notifications

Objective-C encourages loose coupling, and nothing in the Foundation framework better epitomizes this than the *notification* mechanism. Notifications are a simple way of implementing callbacks for arbitrary numbers of listeners.

You can listen for notifications with a specific name, from a specific object, or both. The notification itself has a sender, a name, and a dictionary associated with it, so objects can pass arbitrary amounts of information to things that are listening for notifications.

If you use notifications, you make it very easy to reuse your classes. Rather than expecting every class that wants to listen for events from your classes to implement a particular interface, you just post notifications. Any number of classes can listen for notifications from the same object, and your class doesn't have to implement any of the logic for storing references to them.

Requesting Notifications

```
5   - (void)notify: (NSNotification*)note
6   {
7     NSLog(@"Received %@", note);
8   }
9   - (void)registerListener
10  {
11    NSNotificationCenter *nc =
12      [NSNotificationCenter defaultCenter];
13    [nc addObserver: self
14        selector: @selector(notify:)
15          name: @"Example"
16        object: nil];
17  }
18  - (void)dealloc
19  {
20    NSNotificationCenter *nc =
21      [NSNotificationCenter defaultCenter];
22    [nc removeObserver: self];
23    [super dealloc];
24  }
```

From: notify.m

To listen for notifications, you need to register an interest for them with the **NSNotificationCenter** object for your thread. This is the routing point for notifications. When a notification is posted, it is sent to the notification center and the notification center then forwards it to all of the interested parties.

Most of the time, you will be using the default notification center. It is possible to create different notification centers for different uses, but most commonly you

will use the standard one. This is obtained
by sending a +defaultCenter message to
NSNotificationCenter.

To register for a notification, you then send an
-addObserver:selector:name:object: message
to the center. Note the selector argument in this
message. A single object may receive different
notifications on different methods. This is quite
useful, because it means that you don't need to
test what kind of notification you've received and
can cleanly separate out different event handlers
into different methods.

Either the object or the notification name can be
nil when registering an observer. This lets you
register either to receive all messages sent by a
specific object, or all notifications of a specific
type, irrespective of their sender.

These are more useful for debugging than
anything else. You can, for example, write a
logging aspect that listens for all notifications
of a particular type and logs the sender.

One important thing to remember when you
listen for a notification is that the notification
center does not retain your object. If your object
is still registered to receive notifications when it
is destroyed, then your program will crash the
next time one of these notifications is sent.

To avoid this, make sure that you send the
notification center a -removeObserver: message
in your -dealloc method. If you forget this, the
crash will not be obvious. You will see a lot of

strange things in the back trace, including the
notification center.

Sending Notifications

```
33  NSNotificationCenter *nc =
34    [NSNotificationCenter defaultCenter];
35  [nc postNotificationName: @"Example"
36                    object: @"sender"
37                  userInfo: nil];
```

From: notify.m

Posting notifications is even easier than
registering to listen for them. The canonical way
of posting a notification object is to construct an
NSNotification object and then send it.

In practice, I don't think that I've ever seen code
that does this. The notification center has some
convenience methods that construct and post
notifications in a single operation.

The most common way of
sending a notification is the
-postNotificationName:object:userInfo:
method. There is also a simplified version of
this that omits the **userInfo:** parameter and is
equivalent to passing **nil** as the final parameter.

Note that the object—the sender of the
notification—is specified as a parameter. That
means that it is possible to send notifications
claiming to be from another object. This means
that, for example, façades or C code can send

notifications on behalf of other objects.

Enqueuing Notifications

```
44   NSNotificationQueue *nq =
45     [NSNotificationQueue defaultQueue];
46   NSNotification *note = [NSNotification
47     notificationWithName: @"Example"
48                   object: @"sender"];
49   [nq enqueueNotification: note
50             postingStyle: NSPostWhenIdle];
51   [[NSRunLoop currentRunLoop] run];
```

From: notify.m

Sometimes, your code might be generating a lot of notifications, or may be generating ones that do not need to be handled immediately. The NSNotificationQueue class solves both of these problems.

Notification queues can both defer delivery of notifications and can coalesce them. Unlike NSNotificationCenter, the queue does not have convenience methods for constructing the notifications, you must do this yourself. The notification is then posted with one of three posting styles.

In this example, the notification's delivery is deferred until there are no other events in the run loop. Timers and data becoming ready on file descriptors take priority. Alternatively, you can post in the next run loop iteration or immediately.

If you send a lot of notifications of the same type then it is a good idea to cache the notification object. Passing the same object to the notification queue repeatedly is quite cheap, and it can automatically send the notification just once.

If you use the longer method for queuing notifications, one of the parameters is `coalesceMask:`, which determines how notifications should be combined. You can combine notifications with the same name, notifications with the same sender, or both.

Coalescing is most useful with the `NSPostWhenIdle` posting style. You can send the same notification a lot of times when your code is busy and then, when there are no other events left to handle, the notification queue will post just one copy of the notification. This is ideal for bits of code that trigger some low-priority book-keeping work.

Sending Notifications Between Applications

```
19    [c       addObserver: self
20          selector:
21    @selector(newCopyStarted:)
22            name: ProcessDidStart
23          object: nil
24  suspensionBehavior:
25    NSNotificationSuspensionBehaviorHold];
```

From: distributedNotify.m

The loose coupling provided by notifications is so useful that it is extended within the Foundation framework to provide a (simple) mechanism for communication between applications. The `NSDistributedNotificationCenter` class is a subclass of `NSNotificationCenter` that broadcasts notifications to other applications.

This extension requires some changes. A normal notification has a sender associated with it, which is a pointer to some object. A pointer to an object is not particularly useful in a process with another address space, so distributed notifications use a string as the sender. This can be anything that you like, but it's usually the application name.

Notifications can have dictionaries associated with them. Within an application, these dictionaries can contain any objects, but for broadcast they are restricted to objects that can be stored in *property lists* (see Chapter 9).

Note: On OS X, there is only a single type of distributed notification center, sending notifications to applications owned running with the same user ID as the sender. GNUstep provides two others, one for communicating with all applications on a computer, irrespective of the user, and one for broadcasting notifications across the local network.

The delivery semantics for distributed notifications are also somewhat different. When you post a (normal) notification, it is delivered synchronously. The sending object already has control of the CPU. The stack frame for its method is at the top of the stack and it is free to delegate program flow to the notification center, which then delegates it to the notification listeners.

With a distributed notification, this is not the case. You can't just interrupt whatever another process is doing in the middle of a function[1] and so you must wait until a convenient point.

Distributed notifications handle this by interfacing with the run loop. To receive distributed notifications, you must be using **NSRunLoop**. The distributedNotify.m example is a simple program that writes a log message whenever a new instance of itself is started.

---

[1] Well, you can; signals do exactly that, but the things you can do from a signal handler are quite limited.

```
14   - (id)init
15   {
16     NSDistributedNotificationCenter *c =
17       [NSDistributedNotificationCenter
             defaultCenter];
18
19     [c       addObserver: self
20               selector:
21       @selector(newCopyStarted:)
22                 name: ProcessDidStart
23                 object: nil
24     suspensionBehavior:
25       NSNotificationSuspensionBehaviorHold];
26
27     NSProcessInfo *pinfo =
28       [NSProcessInfo processInfo];
29     NSNumber *pid = [NSNumber numberWithInt:
30       [pinfo processIdentifier]];
31     NSDictionary *userInfo = [NSDictionary
32       dictionaryWithObject: pid
33                    forKey: @"pid"];
34
35     [c postNotificationName: ProcessDidStart
36                    object: [pinfo processName]
37                  userInfo: userInfo
38                  options: 0];
39     [[NSRunLoop currentRunLoop] run];
40   }
```

From: distributedNotify.m

The −init method of this class does all of the
real work. First, it registers an observer for a
distributed notification. The object is nil, so it
will receive this notification from any sender.
Then it constructs the notification. The user
info dictionary contains a single key-value pair

storing the process ID.

After it's posted the notification, it starts
the run loop. The program will then sit in
a blocking state until some run loop events
happen. Only one event has a handler defined
in this program, so all that it will ever do is
receive a `-newCopyStarted:` message whenever a
`ProcessDidStart` notification is posted, which
will only happen when another copy of this
program is run.

If you compile and run this example, you will see
that it receives its own notification, so it will tell
you that it has started. If you run another copy,
you will get a log message from each running
instance telling you about the new one.

This is quite a trivial example, but it's easy to
use distributed notifications for more complex
events. I use them in XMPPKit, for example,
to notify all running applications when the user
changes online state. Other programs listen for
this and can push the new status message to
microblogging sites.

Network Access

The standard cross-platform way of writing network-aware applications is the Berkeley Sockets API. This was written as part of the same grant that developed the TCP/IP and is designed to be protocol-agnostic.

Most languages have an implementation of this API. In Objective-C, you are, as always, free to use the C version, which provides all of the power of the low-level interfaces.

Most of the time, however, this is a lot of effort for very little gain. The Foundation framework provides several classes that make it easier to write networked applications. Using these abstractions sometimes loses you some of the power of the lower-level APIs, but not much.

Wrapping C Sockets

```
42   return
43     [[[NSFileHandle alloc]
44       initWithFileDescriptor: s
45             closeOnDealloc: YES]
46        autorelease];
```

From: NSFileHandle+Socket.m

We looked briefly at the **NSFileHandle** class in Chapter 13 and I mentioned that it wrapped a file descriptor. The socket API was designed based on the UNIX everything-is-a-file-even-when-it-doesn't-make-sense model, so sockets are also file descriptors. You can use the same function calls for reading from and writing to a socket that you can use with any other file descriptor.

You can also use an **NSFileHandle** to wrap a socket. This lets you use the low-level APIs to create a socket to your exact specifications, then use a more abstract way of interacting with the created socket. If you need to use any parts of the low-level socket API that are not conveniently exposed by the higher-level APIs then this is the only solution that you can use. In other cases, it is still often the most convenient one.

The biggest advantage of wrapping your socket in a file descriptor object is that you can easily integrate it with the run loop. This lets you very easily write event-driven socket code. The other

Note: Remember that the aim of Objective-C was to make life easier for C programmers. Don't use Objective-C APIs just for the sake of it, only use them when they make more sense as a solution to your specific problem than the C APIs. Using an Objective-C API that is just a trivial wrapper around the C API adds overhead and complexity, but doesn't make your code any easier to maintain.

big advantage is that you can use Objective-C reference counting for your socket. If you pass **YES** as the argument to the `closeOnDealloc:` argument when you create the `NSFileHandle`, then the file descriptor will be closed when the object is deallocated.

If you send a `-waitForDataInBackgroundAndNotify` message to your object, it will be added to the list of file descriptors that the run loop polls. At the next run loop iteration, if there is data waiting then the `NSFileHandle` object will post a notification. If you have registered a handler for this notification, then you can read the new data.

The documentation for this method is somewhat misleading. It claims that this method will create another thread. In fact, on OS X the run loop uses the `kqueue()` API[1] and calling this

---

[1]GNUstep may use `poll()` or `select()` instead.

method just adds another file descriptor to the list that it waits for. With OS X 10.6, this is implemented using *Grand Central Dispatch* to post the notification, but the core functionality is the same.

One final advantage is that you are freed from thinking about buffers. When you read data from a socket, you typically have to allocate a buffer and then pass a pointer to it to a **read()** or **recv()** system call. With a file descriptor object, you read **NSData** instances.

If you are writing a lot of strings, then you might want to consider adding a category on **NSFileHandle** that provides -**writeUTF8String:** and -**readUTF8String** methods, or equivalent methods for the encoding that your protocol uses, allowing you to get and send strings directly.

Connecting to Servers

```
6    NSInputStream *in;
7    NSOutputStream *out;
8    NSHost *host = [NSHost hostWithName:
9      @"example.com"];
10   [NSStream getStreamsToHost: host
11                         port: 80
12                  inputStream: &in
13                 outputStream: &out];
14   [in open];
```

From: nsstream.m
Objective-C provides a set of Java-like stream

classes for network communication, as well as the low-level UNIX interfaces. Unfortunately, the stream versions are not particularly useful. They don't provide a clean way of adding filters like compression or of negotiating encryption in the middle of a connection, which a lot of modern protocols require.

The most distressing limitation, however, is that they don't make it easy to support SRV records. These are DNS records that advertise a service to port mapping, as well as a hostname to IP address mapping. They are used by DNS-SD, but the IP address shortage makes them increasingly common in hierarchical DNS on the public Internet.

If you look up a server address on OS X using the POSIX `getaddrinfo()` function, then you provide a host name and service name. The system then maps these to network addresses and port numbers on any of the supported protocols.

When you construct an `NSStream`, you must specify the port number as an integer. This means that it will fail on any service that uses DNS SRV records. If you use `getaddrinfo()` and then wrap the resulting socket in an `NSFileHandle`, however, it will work correctly. In EtoileFoundation, we provide a category on `NSFileHandle` that allows you to create file handles directly from a host name and protocol name, wrapping this call.

```
16    hints.ai_family = PF_UNSPEC;
17    hints.ai_socktype = SOCK_STREAM;
18    //Ask for a stream address.
19    error = getaddrinfo(server, service, &hints, &
          res0);
20    if (error) { return nil; }
21
22    int s = -1;
23    for (struct addrinfo *res = res0;
24      res != NULL && s < 0 ;
25      res = res->ai_next)
26    {
27      s = socket(res->ai_family, res->ai_socktype,
28        res->ai_protocol);
29      //If the socket failed, try the next address
30      if (s < 0) { continue ; }
31
32      //If the connection failed, try the next
            address
33      if (connect(s, res->ai_addr, res->ai_addrlen) <
            0)
34      {
35        close(s);
36        s = -1;
37        continue;
38      }
39    }
40    freeaddrinfo(res0);
```

From: NSFileHandle+Socket.m

This category is shown in the
NSFileHandle+Socket.m example. When
you call **getaddrinfo()**, you provide the server
and service type as C strings and a set of hints
indicating the kind of socket that you want. You
then get an array of **addrinfo** structures back,

containing the information required to construct a connected socket.

These are arranged in the order that the resolver thinks is best, so you typically try each on in turn, until you find one that works. If you have both IPv6 and v4 connectivity, then this code will try both if there are DNS entries pointing at both.

Sharing Objects Over a Network

```
6   NSMutableDictionary *object =
7      [NSMutableDictionary new];
8   NSConnection *conn =
9      [NSConnection new];
10  [conn setRootObject: object];
11  if ([conn registerName: @"sharedDict"])
12  {
13     [[NSRunLoop currentRunLoop] run];
14  }
```

From: doPublish.m

One of the most powerful, and most underused, parts of Objective-C is the *distributed objects* system. If you send a message to an object, and the object doesn't understand how to handle it, then it will receive a **-forwardInvocation:** message, with an object encapsulating the message as an argument.

Like everything else in Objective-C, you can introspect this object. It will tell you the selector, the number of arguments, and the types and values of all of the arguments.

The Foundation framework includes a class, **NSDistantObject**, which makes use of this. A distant object is a proxy that forwards messages to a remote object. The remote objects can be in a different process, or even on a different computer.

If you pass objects as arguments to a message sent to a distant object, then they may be copied, or a remote proxy may be created at the far end forwarding message back.

Using distributed objects is very simple. There are two parts of any program that uses them: a client and a server. The server offers objects to other processes and the client connects to the server and accesses them.

By default, objects are just shared on the local machine. To share them across the network, you must use the use **NSSocketPortNameServer** when registering the object.

```
6    NSMutableDictionary *object = (id)[NSConnection
7      rootProxyForConnectionWithRegisteredName:
8        @"sharedDict"
9                                         host: nil];
10   NSLog(@"Object: %@", object);
11   [object setObject: @"aValue"
12            forKey: @"aKey"];
13   NSLog(@"Object: %@", object);
```

From: doAccess.m

The example from the start of this chapter

shows a simple program that shares an
NSMutableDictionary instance between
processes. Note that you must be using
NSRunLoop to serve distributed objects. The
distributed objects system adds the IPC
channel (a Mach port or a socket) used for
communication to the run loop. When another
process sends a message to that port, some data
arrives through that channel and the DO system
is notified.

It then constructs an **NSInvocation** from the
data received and invokes it, then returns the
result.

```
doAccess[85613:903] Object: {
}
doAccess[85613:903] Object: {
    aKey = aValue;
}
```

Output from: doAccess

Finding Network Peers

```
12   NSProcessInfo *pi = [NSProcessInfo processInfo];
13   NSString *name =
14     [NSString stringWithFormat: @"%@/%@",
15       [pi hostName],
16       NSFullUserName()];
17
18   NSNetService *service =
19     [[NSNetService alloc]
20       initWithDomain: @""
21                 type: type
22                 name: name
23                 port: 123];
24   [service publish];
25
26   NSNetServiceBrowser *sb =
27     [NSNetServiceBrowser new];
28   [sb setDelegate: self];
29   [sb searchForServicesOfType: type
30                      inDomain: @""];
```

From: netservice.m

Over the years, lots of protocols have been used for finding services on the local network. Both NetBIOS and AppleTalk were common on local networks until the mid '90s, until they started to be phased out in favor of TCP/IP.

The TCP/IP protocol stack didn't include anything for doing this. The closest it came was the broadcast address. If you send a packet to the broadcast address then it will be sent to everyone on the local segment. This has a lot of problems; it only works on the local physical segment, it's inefficient on modern switched networks, and it's a very low-level approach.

The IETF's ZeroConf working group proposed *multicast DNS (mDNS)* as the solution to this. DNS is a scalable way of publishing mappings. It is most commonly used for mapping from host names to IP addresses, but it can be used for things like telephone numbers, geolocation information, and a host of other things.

With mDNS, individual computers may publish DNS records in the .local domain. This is then used as the foundation for *DNS service discovery (DNS-SD)*, which describes a way of advertising arbitrary services over DNS. You can use this standard with traditional hierarchical DNS too, but it is most useful with mDNS.

The combination of the two standards is often referred to as *Bonjour* and is exposed to Objective-C via the `NSNetService` class. This allows applications to publish DNS-SD records and find all of the records for a particular service.

Lots of applications use this on OS X. Safari uses it to share bookmarks; iChat uses it to find contacts for serverless messaging; iTunes uses it for sharing music; and the system uses it for finding shared folders and printers. If you are writing any kind of networked application, you may find it helpful to advertise to peers using `NSNetService`.

When you advertise a service, you must specify a unique name. If you are using distributed objects, which we'll look at towards the end of this chapter, then you can use this as the name of the object that you are serving, and ignore the DNS-related underpinnings of the Bonjour system. For other things, the port that you publish is often more useful and the name will be something that you will present to users.

You search for peers using the NSNetServiceBrowser class. This is a little bit more tricky to use correctly. Publishing services is synchronous; you send a -publish message to your NSNetService instance and the service is published. Searching is asynchronous and requires a *run loop* to be active.

When you send the search message to the browser, it will transmit a DNS request. It may take a while to get the response back and you probably don't want to stop the user from doing anything while you search, so this method returns immediately.

When it receives a response, this class will send a message to its delegate with a new NSNetService instance describing each server that it finds. It will then keep listening until you send it a -stop message.

In a lot of cases, you will never send this message. You can just leave the browser running in the background for the lifetime of your process and get notifications whenever a new peer pops up on the local network. You can then trigger an update in your user interface showing the new peer. This is what something like iTunes

does, adding new shared playlists to the library
as they appear on the network.

Loading Data from URLs

```
44    [NSAutoreleasePool new];
45    NSArray *args = [[NSProcessInfo processInfo]
          arguments];
46    NSString *target = [args objectAtIndex: 1];
47    NSURL *targetURL = [NSURL URLWithString: target];
48    if (nil == targetURL) { return 1; }
49    NSURLRequest *req = [NSURLRequest requestWithURL:
          targetURL];
50    id delegate = [DownloadDelegate new];
51    NSURLDownload *dl =
52      [[NSURLDownload alloc] initWithRequest: req
53                                    delegate:
                                            delegate];
54    [dl setDestination: [targetURL lastPathComponent]
55        allowOverwrite: YES];
56    [[NSRunLoop currentRunLoop] run];
```

From: wget.m

If you are writing code for a modern Internet-
connected system, then you are likely to
want to fetch data from a remote location
identified by a *uniform resource locator (URL)*.
A URL is a global identifier, with a schema
and some data specific to that schema. The
Foundation framework includes the NSURL class
to encapsulate URLs. This can parse URLs from
strings and give you an abstract representation.

Foundation also includes two classes for fetching
data from URLs. The simpler of the two is

`NSURLDownload`, which encapsulates a download from a remote URL. The more complex is `NSURLConnection`, which provides a lower-level way of handling requests and responses.

The URL loading system is protocol agnostic but expects a request-response format. The request is encapsulated in an `NSURLRequest`, which you then pass to one of these two classes. It makes the connection and sends the request, then provides you with one or more `NSURLResponse` objects in reply.

Out of the box, the Foundation framework can load data from file://, http://, https://, and ftp:// URLs. You can add support for other protocols by implementing an `NSURLProtocol` subclass. It's quite rare to need to do that, but you might, for example, want to implement support for SFTP or similar in such a class. You could then reuse existing code that delegated file access to the URL loading system.

The example at the start of this section shows how to fetch a file from a remote user-specified URL. This uses a delegate class to report progress to the user, although this is not required.

The delegate stores the size of the response, so that it can provide progress reports. If the transfer fails, it will report a localized error message. If it works, it will print one dot to the terminal for every 1% of the download.

The URL loading subsystem is very powerful,

but most of the time you can restrict yourself to just the subset shown in this example. This lets you integrate with simple web services in a very small amount of code.

```objc
3   @interface DownloadDelegate : NSObject
4   {
5     int progress;
6     long long fetched;
7     long long size;
8   }
9   @end
10  @implementation DownloadDelegate
11  - (void)downloadDidBegin: (NSURLDownload*)
        download
12  {
13    NSLog(@"Started downloading");
14  }
15  -   (void)download: (NSURLDownload*)download
16  didReceiveResponse: (NSURLResponse*)response
17  {
18    size = [response expectedContentLength];
19  }
20  -       (void)download: (NSURLDownload*)download
21  didReceiveDataOfLength:(NSUInteger)length
22  {
23    fetched += length;
24    for (int newProgress = (fetched * 100) / size ;
          newProgress > progress ; progress++)
25    {
26      putc('.', stderr);
27    }
28  }
29  - (void)download: (NSURLDownload*)download
30  didFailWithError: (NSError*)error
31  {
32    NSLog(@"Error: %@", [error localizedDescription
          ]);
33    exit(1);
34  }
35  - (void)downloadDidFinish: (NSURLDownload*)
        download
36  {
37    NSLog(@"Finished downloading");
38    exit(0);
39  }
40  @end
```

From: wget.m

18

Debugging Objective-C

There are two sorts of programmers; those that always write perfect code the first time, and those that really exist. If you are in the former category, you can skip this chapter. If you're in the latter category, then there will be times when you will try running your code and discover that it doesn't work perfectly as expected.

This is an irritating experience, but it is a lot less irritating when you can quickly fix the problem. In this chapter, we'll look at some of the techniques for spotting the cause of bugs in Objective-C programs.

Inspecting Objects

```
3   @interface DebugObject : NSObject @end
4   @implementation DebugObject
5   - (NSString*)description
6   {
7     return @"Not a very helpful message";
8   }
9   @end
10  void debug(id anObject) {}
```

From: description.m

Most of the time, when you debug an Objective-C program, you will be using the *GNU debugger (GDB)*, which has some built-in support for Objective-C. If you are using XCode then you are using GDB via a graphical front end. You can access the command-line interface from the Run menu. This is often useful because XCode only provides a GUI for the most common functions of the debugger, not for everything.

Note: Newer versions of XCode use the *LLVM Debugger (LLDB)* instead of GDB. The graphical interfaces are the same and LLDB supports more or less the same features as GDB.

There are two features in GDB that make it well suited to Objective-C. The first is that it comes with simple Objective-C parser and interpreter, so you can write Objective-C expressions in the debugger and inspect variables in that way. The second is the **print-object** command.

```
1  $ gdb ./a.out
2  (gdb) break debug
3  Breakpoint 1 at 0x100000e4d: file description.m,
       line 10.
4  (gdb) r
5  Starting program: a.out
6  Breakpoint 1, debug (anObject=0x100111bc0) at
       description.m:10
7  10   void debug(id anObject) {}
8  (gdb) print anObject
9  $1 = (id) 0x100111bc0
10 (gdb) print-object anObject
11 Not a very helpful message
12 (gdb) print-object [NSObject new]
13 <NSObject: 0x100111c30>
14 (gdb) print-object [anObject class]
15 DebugObject
16 (gdb) print-object [anObject className]
17 DebugObject
18 (gdb) print-object anObject->isa
19 DebugObject
```

Output from: description

This prints an object. It does this by sending
a -**description** message to the object, which
returns an **NSString** describing the object. This
means that it will only work on valid objects. If
you try using this command with objects that
are prematurely deallocated or whose memory is
corrupted then the debugger will either crash, or
catch a segmentation violation signal.

The default implementation of this method,
in **NSObject**, just prints the class name and

address. Various other standard objects implement it in different ways. Collection classes, for example, print their contents in property list format. This example returned a very unhelpful message, but in your code you should try to provide something a bit more helpful.

Recognizing Memory Problems

```
5   id pool = [NSAutoreleasePool new];
6   NSMutableString *str = [NSMutableString
        stringWithString: @"example"];
7   [pool drain];
8   pool = [NSAutoreleasePool new];
9   NSSet *set = [NSSet setWithObject: str];
```

From: prematureDealloc.m

One of the most common problems in Objective-C is premature deallocation. If you omit a –retain message somewhere, then you hang onto a pointer without increasing its reference count. If something else has a reference to it, or it was autoreleased, then this pointer can remain valid for a long time before suddenly becoming invalid.

When the pointer becomes invalid, you will usually get a crash inside objc_msgSend() with the Mac runtime, or objc_msg_lookup() with the GNU runtime. This happens because the runtime tries to look up the method to handle a

message, but the class pointer is now pointing to
something invalid.

```
1   $ gcc -framework Cocoa -g prematureDealloc.m &&
        ./a.out
2   Segmentation fault
3   $ gdb ./a.out
4   (gdb) r
5   Starting program: a.out
6   Program received signal EXC_BAD_ACCESS, Could not
        access memory.
7   Reason: KERN_INVALID_ADDRESS at address: 0
        x00000007a0000010
8   0x00007fff8296111c in objc_msgSend ()
9   (gdb) up 6
10  #6  0x0000000100000eef in main () at
        prematureDealloc.m:9
11  9    NSSet *set = [NSSet setWithObject: str];
12  (gdb) print-object str
13  Program received signal EXC_BAD_ACCESS, Could not
        access memory.
14  (gdb) print *str
15  $2 = {
16    <NSString> = {
17      <NSObject> = {
18        isa = 0x7a0000000
19      }, <No data fields>}, <No data fields>}
20  (gdb) print-object str->isa
21  Cannot access memory at address 0x7a0000000
22  (gdb) quit
23  $ NSZombieEnabled=YES ./a.out
24  a.out[39571:903] *** -[CFString hash]: message
        sent to deallocated instance 0x100112f00
```

Output from: prematureDealloc

You can find the object that was deallocated
quite easily in the debugger by moving up the

stack until you find the message receiver. You can also use the NSZombie class. When the NSZombieEnable environment variable is set, objects won't be deallocated. Instead, they will have their class set to NSZombie, which just logs a message whenever it is sent a message.

Finding the object is, of course, only part of the problem. You also need to work out why it was prematurely freed. Often, you can do this quickly by just looking in the relevant source files and checking all –retain and –release messages. The static analyzer part of clang can (hopefully) do this automatically. If that doesn't work, then try overriding the class's –retain and –release methods, adding a breakpoint on them in the debugger, and looking at where it is really retained and released.

If you are not using automatic reference counting, migrating to it can help. It then becomes the compiler's job to track pointers, and the compiler is generally better at repeatedly applying patterns than you would be. If you are using ARC already, you can try making unsafe unretained pointers weak. This ensures that they are zeroed when the pointee is deallocated and helps you to safely check whether pointers are valid.

Watching Exceptions

```objc
3    int throw(void)
4    {
5      [NSException raise: @"ExampleException"
6                  format: @"Watch this"];
7    }
```

From: throw.m

If you read the documentation on **NSException**, you will see this in the **-raise** method:

> All other methods that raise an exception invoke this method, so set a breakpoint here if you are debugging exceptions.

This was true, until OS X 10.5, and remains true on GNUstep. Unfortunately, on newer versions of OS X it is untrue, which also makes it more effort if you want to write a category that alters the behavior of exception throwing.

Now, the various exception-throwing bits of OS X Foundation use **@throw** directly. This is a tiny bit of syntactic sugar, which calls the **objc_exception_throw()** function. This function then invokes the unwinding library code to run all code in **@finally** blocks and find the correct handler for the exception.

If you set a breakpoint on **objc_exception_throw()**, then you will catch all exceptions, irrespective of how they

```
1  (gdb) break [NSException raise]
2  Breakpoint 1 at 0x51eb851eb14a14
3  (gdb) r
4  Starting program: a.out
5  2010-03-11 14:52:54.519 a.out[39782:a0f] ***
        Terminating app due to uncaught exception '
        ExampleException', reason: 'Watch this'
6  terminate called after throwing an instance of '
        NSException'
7  Program received signal SIGABRT, Aborted.
8  0x00007fff81c3afe6 in __kill ()
9  (gdb) break objc_exception_throw
10 Breakpoint 2 at 0x7fff829660da
11 (gdb) r
12 Starting program: a.out
13 Breakpoint 2, 0x00007fff829660da in
        objc_exception_throw ()
14 (gdb) bt
15 #0  0x00007fff829660da in objc_exception_throw ()
16 #1  0x00007fff81fd0267 in +[NSException raise:
        format:arguments:] ()
17 #2  0x00007fff81fd01f4 in +[NSException raise:
        format:] ()
18 #3  0x0000000100000ea9 in throw () at throw.m:5
19 #4  0x0000000100000eca in main () at throw.m:12
```

Output from: throw

are thrown. This will also catch things like
@throw @*"string"*; which are not officially
supported on OS X, but still work.

Asserting Expectations

```objc
3  @interface IgnoreAsserts : NSAssertionHandler
4  @end
5  @implementation IgnoreAsserts
6  - (void)handleFailureInFunction: (NSString*)
          functionName
7                     file: (NSString*)fileName
8           lineNumber: (NSInteger)line
9          description: (NSString *)format, ...
10 {
11   NSLog(@"Ignoring assert on line %d of %@() in %
          @", line, functionName, fileName);
12 }
13 @end
14
15 int main(void)
16 {
17   [NSAutoreleasePool new];
18   [[[NSThread currentThread] threadDictionary]
19     setObject: [[IgnoreAsserts new] autorelease]
20        forKey: NSAssertionHandlerKey];
21   NSCAssert(1 == 2, @"This might not be true");
22   return 0;
23 }
```

From: assert.m

In C code, the standard library provides an
assert() macro, which logs a message and calls
abort() when the predicate argument evaluates
to false. The Objective-C versions are slightly
more useful.

Foundation provides two macros, **NSAssert()**
and **NSCAssert()**. If you are using C99
(which you should be) then these are variadic,
otherwise you will need to use the variants,

like **NSAssert1()**, that take fixed numbers of arguments. **NSAssert()** references **self** and so can only be used in an Objective-C method body. **NSCAssert()** can be used in C functions.

Unlike the C variants, these do not abort when the assertion is false. Instead, they send a message to a per-thread assertion handler object. This object is, by default, an instance of **NSAssertionHandler** and throws an **NSInternalConsistencyException** when you hit an assertion. You can catch this and recover, but most often it will reach the top of the stack and cause the program to abort.

You can create your own subclass of **NSAssertionHandler** and override one or both of the assertion-handling methods if you want some other behavior. This example ignores assertions in C functions, just logging a message when they are encountered.

```
1  $ ./a.out
2  a.out[40031:903] Ignoring assert on line 21 of
       main in $@
```

Output from: assert

It's quite unusual to want to override this, but there are some good reasons why you might. One of the most obvious is error reporting. When an assertion is encountered, it means that something has gone badly wrong with your program. You may want to collect some information about the conditions that cause this and upload it to a bug-tracking system, rather than just crash.

You can disable asserts by defining the NS_BLOCK_ASSERTS macro. This is generally only worth doing in performance-critical code. It's usually better to waste a little bit of CPU time than it is to continue in an undefined state.

Logging Debug Messages

```
7   - (void)log
8   {
9       NSLog(@"%s:%d:%s (%@) Log message", __FILE__,
            __LINE__, __PRETTY_FUNCTION__, self);
10  }
```

From: nslog.m

We've used the NSLog() function in quite a bit of code already. When you run an application in the terminal, messages passed to NSLog() go to the standard error stream. On OS X, NSLog() in graphical applications sends messages to the system console. On Microsoft Windows, with GNUstep, they go to the system event monitor.

The NSLog() function writes a format string, prepended by the date, time, process name, and process ID. When you put the %@ format specifier in a format string, it uses exactly the same method as the debugger to get a string representation of the object.

Note: The GNUstep Additions framework
provides a set of logging macros, the
NSDebugLog() family. These wrap NSLog()
but only log when a specific value is set in
user defaults. These make it very easy to turn
debug logging on and off on a per-aspect or per-
framework basis.

You can also use the special macros that
the compiler defines when constructing the
format string. The __FILE__ macro is a C
string containing the name of the current
source file. The __LINE__ macro is an integer
containing the current line number. Finally, the
__PRETTY_FUNCTION__ macro expands to a C
string containing the current method or function
name.

```
1   ./a.out
2   2010-03-11 15:57:43.200 a.out[40861:903] nslog.m
        :9:-[Log log] (<Log: 0x100112b70>) Log
        message
```

Output from: nslog

The Objective-C Runtime

As I said at the start of this book, an Objective-C implementation consists of two parts: the compiler and the runtime library. The compiler takes source code and turns the dynamic bits into calls to the runtime library.

The runtime library is written in C, which means that it is written in a subset of Objective-C. All of the interfaces to the runtime library, including the ones that are called by code generated by the compiler, are accessible to Objective-C code.

Everything dynamic in Objective-C is implemented by the runtime library. The most obvious example of this is message sending. When you send a message, the runtime is responsible for deciding what should handle it.

This is not the only responsibility of the runtime library. It also handles all of the introspection

features of the language. It keeps track of all of
the class and protocol metadata and exposes this
to programmers.

When you use key-value coding, you are
(indirectly) using Objective-C runtime functions
to look up methods and instance variables on the
receiver.

Sending Messages by Name

```
5   id obj = [NSObject new];
6   SEL sel =
7     NSSelectorFromString(@"release");
8   IMP release = [obj methodForSelector: sel];
9   release(obj, sel);
```

From: methodByName.m

Objective-C methods are C functions that
are called via an indirection layer. Exactly
how this is implemented varies a bit between
runtimes. With the NeXT and Apple runtimes,
simple message sends are implemented using the
objc_msgSend() function.

Unfortunately, this is not the only function
that you need. This function is declared as
returning an **id** and will work with any kind of
method that has the same calling convention.
On Darwin/x86, for example, object pointers
are returned in the **eax** register. If you return a
floating point value, it is returned in a floating
point register. If you return a structure, space
for it is allocated in the caller and a pointer is

passed in as a hidden argument.

You have to remember to call either `objc_msgSend_sret()` or `objc_msgSend_fpret()`. This is quite messy, because it means that you have to be aware of the calling conventions on your target platform.

With the GNU runtimes, this is much simpler. There is no `objc_msgSend()` function. Instead, you call `objc_msg_lookup()` and then call the returned function pointer, after casting it to the correct types.

The easiest way of doing this that is portable between runtimes is to use the `-methodForSelector:` method on `NSObject`. This returns a pointer to the function used to implement the method, which you can then call. This takes two hidden arguments; the receiver and the selector.

This is almost enough to call a method by name. The missing part is some mechanism for turning strings into selectors. The `NSSelectorFromString()` function does exactly this. It takes an `NSString` as an argument and returns a selector. You can then pass this to `-methodForSelector:`, and as the second argument to the returned function.

Finding Classes by Name

```
6    Class nsview = NSClassFromString(@"NSView");
7    if (Nil == nsview)
8    {
9      NSLog(@"Not linked against AppKit");
10   }
11   else
12   {
13     id view = [nsview new];
14     NSLog(@"View: %@", view);
15   }
```

From: weakClass.m

One of the runtime's responsibilities is storing a table of all loaded classes. You can enumerate this table, looking at every class in turn, or you can use it to look up a class by name.

The latter is particularly useful for implementing *weak class references*. These are supported directly by the Modern Apple runtime, but the support is not yet exposed via the language, so it's not particularly useful. The idea behind a weak class reference is that you can optionally use a class.

You might, for example, write some code in a framework that used Foundation classes and could use AppKit classes if you linked against AppKit. This framework would then work anywhere that had a Foundation implementation, but would take advantage of AppKit features if they were available. You can also use this mechanism to avoid a dependency on third-party frameworks.

```
1  $ gcc -framework Foundation -g -std=c99 weakClass
      .m && ./a.out
2  a.out[53194:903] Not linked against AppKit
3  $ gcc -framework Cocoa -g -std=c99 weakClass.m &&
        ./a.out
4  a.out[53184:903] View: <NSView: 0x1001163b0>
```

Output from: weakClass

Note the difference in outputs when this example
is linked against Cocoa (which links against
AppKit and Foundation) and just Foundation. If
the NSView class is present, it creates an instance
of it. If it isn't, then it just logs a message.

You can also use this in code that must be
backwards-compatible with old versions of a
framework. If you look up new classes using this
mechanism then you get a Nil value that you
can handle when they are not present.

Testing If an Object
Understands a Method

```
12  SEL sel = @selector(delegateMethod:);
13  if ([delegate respondsToSelector: sel])
14  {
15    [delegate delegateMethod: self];
16  }
```

From: respondsToSelector.m

Objective-C code tends to make use of *informal*

protocols. These are groups of messages that a delegate may, optionally, implement.

When you write code that uses them, you need to test whether the class actually implements the method before sending it.

Note: This isn't quite true. You can just send the message in an **@try** block and catch the exception that's thrown if it doesn't understand the method. Given the cost of throwing exceptions, however, this is not a recommended approach.

Fortunately, this is very simple to do. **NSObject** implements a **–respondsToSelector:** method that tests whether the receiver can handle messages with a given selector.

This method is not just implemented by **NSObject**, it's also part of the **NSObject** protocol. Other root classes will also implement it. This is very important for forwarding.

This method, in **NSObject**, calls the **class_respondsToSelector()** runtime function. In other classes, the implementation is different. If you use the runtime functions directly, then you will have quite fragile code.

Most of the time, you want to know whether the object that you are going to send the message to can handle the message, not whether it has a method that handles the message. These are the same in some languages, such as C++, but in Objective-C they are very different concepts.

When you send a `-respondsToSelector:`
message to a proxy, it will test whether the real
object has a method for that selector. The object
wrapped by the proxy might be yet another
proxy, which will then forward the request.

You can also test for protocol conformance by
sending a `-conformsToProtocol:` message to a
class. Note that this only tests whether the class
was declared as adopting the protocol. Classes
can adopt protocols without implementing all
of their methods (although they shouldn't),
but more commonly classes can implement all
of the methods in a protocol without explicitly
conforming to the protocol.

Forwarding Messages

```
3   @interface Facade : NSObject
4   {
5     id delegate;
6   }
7   @end
8   @implementation Facade
9   - (id)forwardingTargetForSelector: (SEL)aSel
10  {
11    return delegate;
12
13  }
14  - (void)forwardInvocation: (NSInvocation*)anInv
15  {
16    [anInv invokeWithTarget: delegate];
17  }
18  @end
```

From: forward.m

Messages in Objective-C are intended to be similar to Smalltalk messages, rather than C functions. They are late-bound and can be introspected. At the lowest level, they are implemented using C functions, but this is an implementation detail. You can pretend that messages are objects that are passed between other objects, introspected, and then handled by methods.

When you send a message to an object that does not correspond to a method on that object, there are still some ways for the object to handle it. These have evolved a lot over the life of Objective-C.

In old Objective-C code, the object's `-forward::` method was called. This was a variadic method and required the receiver to know the structure of the stack frame. NeXT replaced this with `-forwardInvocation:`. This method is passed an object that encapsulates the message send.

The `-forwardInvocation:` mechanism is very flexible, but it does not have particularly good performance. Creating the object and deconstructing the stack frame costs several hundred times more than a normal message send, meaning that you shouldn't use this mechanism in anything even vaguely performance-critical.

If you use this forwarding mechanism, then you must implement a `-methodSignatureForSelector:` method. This returns an object that represents the structure of the call frame associated with the message. The `NSInvocation` class will use this when creating an object encapsulating the message.

With 10.5, Apple introduced a new, faster, forwarding mechanism. If your object implements a `-forwardingTargetForSelector:` method, this will be called with the selector for the missing method. It can then return an object, and the message will be delivered to that object instead.

This makes things like the façade pattern very easy. You can quickly delegate any method

> **Note:**   The two-stage message-sending
> mechanism used by the GNU runtime does not
> support this new mechanism, and neither do
> old versions of the Apple runtime. If you use it,
> it is a good idea to provide fallback code using
> –forwardInvocation:. If you are using a recent
> Apple runtime, or the GNUstep runtime with the
> non-fragile ABI, you will get the benefit of extra
> speed. If not, then your code will still work, it will
> just be slow.

that you don't understand to your delegate.
If you need to do some extra handling before
or after calling a delegate method, then just
implement that method and call the delegate
method explicitly.

Finding Classes

```
9   int classCount =
10     objc_getClassList(NULL, 0);
11   Class *classList =
12     calloc(classCount, sizeof(Class));
13   objc_getClassList(classList,
14       classCount);
15   for (int i=0 ; i<classCount ; i++)
16   {
17     [classes addObject:
18       NSStringFromClass(
19         classList[i])];
20   }
21   free(classList);
22   [classes sortUsingSelector:
23       @selector(compare:)];
```

From: classTree.m

There are two ways of finding an Objective-C class. If you know the name, then you can just use the **NSClassFromString()** function. This takes a string object as the argument and returns the class, or **Nil** if there is no registered class with that name.

If you don't know the name of the class, then you need to do something different. There are a few cases when you might want to know a class but do not already know its name. For example, if you have a plugin architecture, then you might allow the user to specify bundles to load and then want to collect all of the subclasses of a particular class, or all of the classes that conform to a given protocol.

Note: When you are testing classes for protocol conformance, it's a good idea to use the runtime functions, rather than sending them a +conformsToProtocol: message. Lots of classes use +initialize for lazy initialization, and sending them a message will cause this code to be run even if you aren't actually using the class.

The objc_getClassList() function will give you an array of classes. This takes two pointers as arguments, one is the array that will be used to return the classes, the other is the size of the buffer. If you call it with NULL as the first argument, then it won't return any classes, but it will let you know how many there are.

Once you have this array, you can iterate over it and inspect the classes. In this example, I just store the class names in an array and then sort it. In the next section, you'll see how to take the class names and print the instance variables and methods for each class.

If you were searching for classes that conform to a specific protocol, then you would instead use the **class_conformsToProtocol()** function. This will tell you whether the class conforms to the specified protocol. If it does, then you can add it to the list of loaded plugins.

Inspecting Classes

```
26    const char *name = [className UTF8String];
27    printf("%s\n\tIvars:\n", name);
28    Class cls = NSClassFromString(className);
29    unsigned int ivarCount;
30    Ivar *ivars =
31      class_copyIvarList(cls, &ivarCount);
32    for (unsigned int i=0 ; i<ivarCount ; i++)
33    {
34      printf("\t\t%s\n", ivar_getName(ivars[i]));
35    }
36    free(ivars);
37    unsigned int methodCount;
38    Method *methods =
39      class_copyMethodList(cls, &methodCount);
40    printf("%s\n\tMethods:\n", name);
41    for (unsigned int i=0 ; i<methodCount ; i++)
42    {
43      printf("\t\t%s\n",
44          sel_getName(method_getName(methods[i])));
45    }
```

From: classTree.m

Once you have a pointer to a class, either
by enumerating all classes, sending a
-class message to an object, or using
NSClassFromString(), you can inspect it. The
class structure contains a lot of information
about Objective-C classes, all of which is
available to the programmer.

With older runtimes, **Class** was a **typedef** for
struct objc_class, which was defined in a
header. On more modern systems, **Class** is an
opaque type and you are expected to interact
with it via a set of public functions. This makes

it easier to evolve the ABI over time. The layout of the class structure can be changed just by modifying the compiler and runtime, without needing changes to any other code.

The classTree.m example prints the instance variables and methods for all of the classes in the system. There is a lot more metadata that you can access. For example, instance variables store their type and the offset from the start of the object.

This information is used in the implementation of KVC. When you set a value for a key, and KVC is permitted to directly access instance variables, then it will first find an instance variable with the matching name. It will then find the type and determine whether it needs to unbox the object. Finally, it will add the ivar offset to the object pointer and then perform the assignment at this address.

It does something similar with accessor methods. Methods store their name, their types, and their method pointer. The type information is important, because it allows other code to construct a call frame. By checking the types of an accessor method, the KVC code can cast the method pointer to the correct type and then call it, setting or getting a particular property.

With the newer runtimes, there is metadata stored for declared properties as well. Almost anything that you set about a class can be inspected by calling runtime functions. The only thing that you can't do is retrieve the source code for individual methods.

Creating New Classes

```objc
#include <objc/runtime.h>

id fakeDealloc(id self, SEL _cmd, ...)
{
  NSLog(@"%@ sent a -dealloc message", self);
}

void makeIndestructible(id obj)
{
  Class new =
    objc_allocateClassPair(obj->isa, "Fake", 0);
  class_addMethod(new, @selector(dealloc),
      fakeDealloc, "v@:");
  objc_registerClassPair(new);
  obj->isa = new;
}
```

From: newClass.m

Creating new classes at run time is quite rare, but it does provide a lot of opportunities for very dynamic behavior or optimization. We already looked at a bit of the Foundation framework that does this. The key-value observing mechanism creates new classes to intercept accessor method calls.

The most important thing about creating classes at run time is that it demonstrates one of the core principles of Objective-C; that nothing the compiler does is magic. You can generate in your own C code everything that the compiler generates from Objective-C code. Of course, the compiler will probably do a better job of optimizing the result, and the Objective-C version will be simpler. If this were not the case, there wouldn't be much point in Objective-C.

Creating a new class involves three steps. First you allocate the class pair, then you add methods, instance variables, and protocols, and finally you register the class pair with the runtime.

Note: The term class pair can seem confusing. Every Objective-C class in your source code is compiled to two classes at run time. An object is an instance of the class, and the class is an instance of the *metaclass*. Instance methods are attached to the class and class methods are attached to the metaclass. When you send a message to the class, the metaclass is used to look up the corresponding method.

When you allocate the class pair, you must provide the superclass, the name of the new class, and the amount of space added on the end of the class structure. The name of the new class must be unique. The example code for this section will not work if you call the function twice. The simplest way of working around this is to keep a counter in a static variable, increment it atomically every time that you create a new class, and append it to the class name string.

The extra space on the end of the class can be very useful when you combine class creation with *isa-swizzling*. Changing the `isa` pointer of an existing class lets you add methods, but not instance variables. You can, however, create some space on the end of the class structure and store extra data there. Calling `object_getIndexedIvars()` with the class as the argument will give you the address of the start of this data.

You can use this functionality to implement other object models. I've used it, for example, to add prototype-based object orientation to Objective-C, allowing closures to be used as methods and added to a single object.

Adding New Instance Variables

```
2   #include <objc/runtime.h>
3
4   @interface NSObject (Annotated)
5   - (NSString*)annotation;
6   - (void)setAnnotation: (NSString*)aString;
7   @end
8   static char key;
9   @implementation NSObject (Annotated)
10  - (NSString*)annotation
11  {
12    return objc_getAssociatedObject(self, &key);
13  }
14  - (void)setAnnotation: (NSString*)aString
15  {
16    objc_setAssociatedObject(self, &key, aString,
        OBJC_ASSOCIATION_RETAIN);
17  }
18  @end
19
20  int main(void)
21  {
22    [NSAutoreleasePool new];
23    id obj = [NSDictionary new];
24    [obj setAnnotation: @"A note"];
25    NSLog(@"Annotation: %@", [obj annotation]);
26    return 0;
27  }
```

From: associate.m

Starting with OS X 10.6, the Objective-C runtime provides a mechanism that allows you to—almost—add new instance variables to existing classes. There are two functions, used for storing *associative references* to objects. These are object pointers that are associated with the object, after its creation.

Adding new instance variables is not possible after an object has been created, because its memory layout is fixed by this point, but associative references are the next best thing. The example at the start of this section shows a category on NSObject that demonstrates this capability. It allows you to associate a string value with any object, via a pair of methods.

There are two things to note about the functions for setting and getting associative references. The first is the key. This has to be a unique pointer value, not used by any other code to identify a different associative reference. The simplest way of doing this is to define some static variable in the file and use its address.

The other thing to note is the association policy. These policies mirror those available for declared properties. In this case, we're telling the runtime to retain the object now and to release it when the object is destroyed.

There are some cases where associative references are very useful, especially when debugging. If you use the retain policy, the associated object will be released when the object that it is associated with is deallocated, so you can use a block to log a message about the deallocation, for example, without having to modify the object that you are deallocating. You can also use it to easily differentiate two objects, for example, by adding a note indicating where they were created via a category like the one in the example. Be aware, however, that associative references are quite expensive. If you make heavy use of them in production code, don't be surprised if your code becomes very slow.

Index